Guiding Grace

Wisdom of the
Silver Sisters

Authored and Compiled by

Sandy Rogers and Sharyn G. Jordan

Guiding Grace

Wisdom of the Silver Sisters

Authored and Compiled by

Sandy Rogers and Sharyn G. Jordan

Goodyear, AZ

Table of Contents

Dedication

Dedicated to our divine Wisdom of the Silver Sisterhood, a community of Women Writers who are Guided by Grace itself. To our spunky and spiritual Poets, Brave-HeARTs, Sages, Muses, and dynamic Difference-Makers whose up-leveled choices, deeds, and voices create transformational alchemy. To our glorious Goddesses, who challenge one another to Rise Up in the world and elevate awareness. Thank you for cultivating an enriched culture of Way-Showers, who are profoundly courageous Pioneers and Influencers who birth positive, Social Change. Merci, for BEing the Super Shero who boldly answered the greatest call of all: Your Highest Destiny.

"People often think of the Goddess as a fertility deity only.
Not at all – she is the muse.
She is the inspirer of poetry.
She is the inspirer of the spirit.
So, she has three functions: one, to give us life;
two, to be the one who receives us in death;
and three, to inspire our spiritual, poetic realization."

~ Joseph Campbell
Goddess: Mysteries of the Feminine Divine

Preface

Wisdom of the Silver Sisters, Guiding Grace cordially invites you to adventure into our delightfully *ECLECTIC* and magical journey of the heart.

Our brave authors' experiential stories have shown up as the joys of whimsy, the admirable discipline of unfolding professional profoundness, a daughter's last gift, and granddaughter's treasured red box – the power of legacy, the despair of brokenness that led to healing, and even time travel.

We **Silver Sisters** are the creative Sheroes who did not allow society to dictate our path. Instead, we looked to *Grace* in all its glory, gladness, and gratitude to be our **Guide**. We applaud our authors, our fellow Silver Sisters; as we know, writing takes courage, is transformational, and leaves in its wondrous wake *Wisdom*.

Each chapter is compelling, inspirational and although you will resonate with most, the ones that are foreign to your life so far, we invite you to be bold and step into the multiverse of their remarkably radiant and, yes, diverse universe. For those authors with whom you relate, please reach out, get to know them, and enrich your own Shero Journey.

Indeed, *Grace* is the intentional flow and the divine focus of encouragement, integrity, and regard for all humanity.

Deep Bow

Sandy Rogers and Sharyn G. Jordan
Authors and Co-Compilers
Wisdom of the Silver Sisters, Guiding Grace

Prologue

Welcome to our ***Wisdom of the Silver Sisters, Guiding Grace.*** This profound book promises to overflow your CUPPA with *divine* joy, wonder, and awe. Since its inception in November 2020, our stellar storybook continues to unfold *divine* magic. I am blessed, honored, and ecstatic to introduce forty-five insightful, intuitive, innovative, and wisdom-rich authors whose inspirational stories comprise a deeply meaningful anthology. By the way, the operative word is *divine,* which is indicative of supremely great and good; plus, it is spiritually relevant in perfectly describing our Shero-Writers.

You will relish in the magical way our ***Silver Sisters*** book idea came to life. Yet, first, permit me to *divinely* acknowledge my esteemed colleague, co-compiler, and co-author, Sandy Rogers. When I asked her to BE my partner in such a sublime, mighty mission, immediately she said, "YES!" Sandy has given every part of her luminous skill sets, extensive business modeling, professional net-weaving, and loving focus to ***Wisdom of the Silver Sisters, Guiding Grace's*** book project. Indeed, our entire nurturing process continues to BE Exhilarating. Our initial step was to set intentional integrity -- essential to our hours and hours of building a strong foundation. We felt the magic of this idea inspiring and continue to BE Humbled in holding space for such remarkable authors. As Sandy and I co-created guideline documents, crafted invitations enthusiastically conveying the sheer joy of this unique platform, managed wise cost-structures, pondered and poured over thematic considerations, evaluated reasonable timelines, and much, much more, this project continues to BE D*ivine*. I am yin to Sandy's yang, who is an incredible blessing!

Organically, the sacred book process just became better and better. Early on, Sandy introduced me to the brilliant Becky Bee Norwood, founder of – ta-da, drum roll please – Spotlight Publishing. Singing Book-Master Becky's praises is pure bliss as she has personally taken over three-hundred books to Amazon's coveted Best-Selling Book status. Synchronicity was certainly fulfilled as you will soon read of the significance of her company's name. Indeed, our *divine* book was now in great, good helping hands. Then two more angels came on board per our award-winning photographer, Florine Duffield, and editor-extraordinaire, Norma-Jean Strickland. Do read their glorious chapters. Altogether, in perfect and *divine* order, everyone fulfilled an inspirationally far-reaching vision. Thank you!

As promised, the history behind the scenes: Going back to the summer of 2020, Sandy invited me to BE a contributing author in the lovely *Love Meets Life* collaborative book, compiled by the amazing Tara Ijai. The inspired interactions, unwavering support, and celebration of those stories was most impactful. At the time, I was in-the-midst of writing a treasured family trilogy; immersed in the value of preserving the magic of story. On the very night of our mid-autumn *Love Meets Life*'s in-person book-signing (rare for the guarded timeline), I dreamed of the Silver Sister's book project. It appeared as a BE-Dazzling, spectacular spotlight shining on wise women Writerlies. Those bright souls ready to BE Seen, way-showers who exquisitely elevate, edify, and exemplify walking in beauty, grace, and gratitude. Upon asking the dream after the community's name, I was shown a storybook entitled, ***Wisdom of the Silver Sisters, Guiding Grace***. In my bones, I knew bold, brave, and courageous authors, aka alchemists who are BEing the Difference, would valiantly join in.

Circling back to the dream, it was then the *divine* book seeds were planted in the fertile soil of abundance. The next morning, I began holding sacred space to fulfill the vision of shining a Spotlight upon each author, their gifts of story, and our community. My daily one-and-a-half-hour practice continues to cultivate this *divine* growth process. I also knew having a partner would BE *Divine.* Since the energy fueling the Silver Sister's project was gaining momentum, I prayed for guidance. Within a few days, I awoke to "see" the name of the exemplary Sandy Rogers "written" on my ceiling. I was elated! In retrospect, our deep and wide learning curves, laughter – and, yes, a few tears – have been invaluable.

Please prepare to BE Inspired, get comfy, have your CUPPA nearby and drink in our sacred storytellers' legends, legacies, and family folklore. May our magical, meaningful, and muse-worthy stories enrich your experiential journey called life. I believe it will inspire you to scribe your personal S/Hero tales as they will indeed blossom into true and lasting self-love, self-confidence, and self-acceptance. For us, they have gifted a keener clarity, an even greater capaciousness of spirit, and created a *divine* connection to the sumptuously sacred space between the inner and outer worlds. We send this soul-filled storybook forth as a BE-Jeweled Blessing to effect equanimity, empathy and to create an effusive Tao of Exquisite Living.

Deep Bow,
Sharyn G. Jordan, Author
Home Whisperer, Feng Shui Simplified Consultancy, founded 1994
Honored Co-Compiler of *Wisdom of the Silver Sisters, Guiding Grace*

Why This Book

While you may think the title of this book implies that it is a book about women who have matured (another word for "old") and their hair has turned silver, you would be partially correct.

For this book, we define "a Silver Sister" as a woman who, from the age of a toddler to the present time, has amassed many experiences and gained much knowledge. That knowledge creates a Pearl of deep and profound Wisdom.

Wisdom of the Silver Sisters, Guiding Grace is a book co-authored by 45 dynamic women, ranging in age from their 20s to their 80s. Their stories are ones of joy, tears, beauty, and tragic experiences that brought them wisdom in various ways.

The inspiration for this book came from an experience that my co-author, Sharyn G. Jordan, and I had when we both contributed our respective chapters to another collaborative book. Shortly after the launch of that book, Sharyn came to me and asked if I would like to partner with her in a collaborative book she had already entitled, *Wisdom of the Silver Sisters, Guiding Grace.* I immediately knew it was right for me.

Sharyn and I are opposites. However, we complement one another in a synchronistic way. She is a creative, right-brain, earth-mother who has authored several other books, traveled extensively, and owned many successful businesses. And, while I do have a creative side, I am the more left-brain, detail-oriented one. I, too, have an entrepreneurial spirit and have founded several successful businesses.

We are two women born in 1948, and in the year 2021 (this year), we will reach the young age of 73. Starting a new, detail-oriented project was not on my bucket list at age 73. However, this project speaks to my heart, as well as my passion for bringing people together.

With our decision to partner in this project, we knew we needed the services of a professional publisher. We decided to engage the services of a woman I have known for over 20 years, Becky Norwood with Spotlight Publishing. That decision is the reason you are reading this book. We can't find enough glowing adjectives to describe our incredible journey with her. Thank you, Becky!

Initially, Sharyn and I said we would invite women over 55 to join us in this project. You know the phrase, "There are no accidents"? Well, let me tell you a quick story.

In the Greater Phoenix, Arizona area, I am known as "The Referral Queen" due to my many years working as an entrepreneur serving others who work in the holistic, metaphysical, and spiritual fields and my ability to connect others for business or personal needs. I have a large database of people.

When I created an email group to announce we were seeking women over 55 to consider participating in this book, I "accidentally" added a group of people from another project that included men, as well as women, who I knew were not 55. The responses from some of the men were pretty comical. What is important here is that I received responses from several women who said they were not even close to 55, but who said they wanted to be part of this book.

When Sharyn and I talked about it, we realized that wisdom doesn't begin at a certain age or when we have silver hair. Wisdom comes from having experiences that create a nugget of knowledge. Through that knowledge, the Pearl of Wisdom is revealed.

With this knowledge, Sharyn and I realized that we were limiting what this book could bring to those who read these stories. We announced that this was open to any woman who felt a calling to share their story about wisdom and grace. The result of that decision is the 45 chapters of this book.

Once we made that decision, there was so much magic that began showing up! Women we had not been in touch with reached out asking to be part of this project. Some of those women brought gifts and skills to this project which were needed resources. One of our authors is a professional photographer who offered her services to our Sisters. Another is an Emmy award-winning celebrity ghostwriter and editor, who also provided her services to our Sisters. Yet another is a business consultant who offered to put together our corporation (Triangulus 3 Publishing, LLC). The list could go on for pages. Suffice it to say, this has been a magical journey that all 45 women have experienced.

Our deepest desire is that you will find each of these stories inspiring, uplifting, informative, and relatable in some way. We invite you to share this book with others. And, most of all, thank you for holding this book in your hands.

In Gratitude and Appreciation!
Sandy Rogers, Entrepreneur, Consultant, Author
Ask Sandy Rogers, LLC
Co-Compiler of Wisdom of the Silver Sisters, Guiding Grace

Foreword

By Hafsa Kamara

Women are the foundation of life. Sisterhood is the foundation of an everlasting bond.

My first lesson about sisterhood came from a tiny, stubbornly loving woman I have the pleasure of calling Thame (keep reading to find out who Thame is). During my elementary school days, my Thame came to stay with us from Sierra Leone. Her petite stature was no match for her fiery, stubborn personality. She was your typical Thame in many ways, and she was unlike anyone you've ever met. A woman of great knowledge who spoke every tribal language in Sierra Leone, but for the life of her couldn't remember her own birthday! (During her lifetime, most children were born at home, so very few records of births were kept.)

When I was a kid, my Thame was a wonder to behold. Everything about her left me curious and wanting to know more. From her clothes to her mannerisms to even her name – Thame. One day, I mustered up the courage to ask her, "Granny, what does Thame mean?"

She replied, "Thame is Temne for sister."

"Wait, what?! Your first name means sister?"

"No, my first name is Haja Aminata, but everyone calls me Thame, even my children and grandchildren."

That took my young mind for a loop! How can children refer to their mother as sister? Even me; I've been calling my grandma sister this whole time! I felt ashamed as if I was belittling her role as my grandmother and the leader of our family by calling her sister.

I told her calling her sister doesn't seem right because she's more than a sister to me.

Thame responded by saying, "Being your sister in life is more than anything else to me. Right now, you are a child, and what you know about family, friends, teachers, and others is molded in concrete for you. Over time, you will learn that family doesn't have to carry your blood or name, friends are always near even when they are far, and you can learn from a child just as much as you learn from a professor. Yes, as the mother of your mother, I am known to you as grandma, and I love being your grandma. But I am also your sister. As your sister, we share a space of womanhood, a place of empathy, sacrifice, and strength. As your sister, I see you as more than a granddaughter but as a woman-to-be, a wife-to-be, a mother-to-be. I see you as another pillar of this foundation that is needed in our community. As a sister, I see me in you, and I know my legacy will go beyond the blood we share. It'll be in the bond we share as sisters in life."

Wisdom of the Silver Sisters shares the stories of our sisters in life in a way where we can see ourselves in them. My Thame made it apparent to me that your sisters are everywhere in life, from the ones you grew up with to the ones you will meet in this book today. Each author of *Wisdom of the Silver Sisters* shares a unique experience on the journey of failure to redemption, devastating loss to a salubrious rising, a moment of empowerment, connection, fortitude, strength, and unwavering bravery. From this book, you will find that you are not alone in your journey. You will learn through the stories of your sisters to embrace the lows of life as a guiding light toward the highs. You will wonder if you are capable of such strength – YOU ARE. You will wonder if you can overcome your difficulties as your sisters have – YOU CAN. You will wonder if it is possible to be part of such a sisterhood – YOU ALREADY ARE.

If you take a lesson from *Wisdom of the Silver Sisters*, it is that YOUR STORY MATTERS. Your experiences have provided you with a wisdom that only you can speak from. Reading the stories of these amazing authors will empower you to tap into your contribution to life's foundation. I welcome you to see yourself in your sister's shoes. I challenge you to be involved in your sister's journey. I encourage you to share your own journey.

As grandma Thame would say, "Your sister's journey is just as much yours as it is hers." *Wisdom of the Silver Sisters* is all of our stories.

Hafsatu Kamara

Hafsatu Kamara is a 2016 Rio Olympian and entrepreneur in the digital marketing space who advocates for women's and girls' rights and education for all, especially for those based in West Africa.

Born in Virginia in the United States to Sierra Leonean parents, Hafsatu has spent most of her life traveling the globe competing in various track and field competitions, which has given her unique insight into people and the world. Hafsatu volunteers her time and expertise on numerous boards, including DreamWakers, A.R.C. - Active, Resolute, Connected, and DoAm4Salone.

She's going into her fifth year with the Consultment Agency team lead by Wisdom of the Silver Sisters co-author, Chelsea Sutton. Therein she met Sharyn G. Jordan-Hathcock, one of the co-compilers of Wisdom of the Silver Sisters author. Hafsatu credits the presence of both women in her life for a positive upward trajectory in her career and for creating a loving space to learn.

Hafsa is currently based in Los Angeles. She believes that everyone has a unique voice with a story to tell. To like-minded individuals who aspire to be known for more than just one role in life, she would say, "Be proud of the many hats you wear and rule the world!"

Hafsa enjoys spending time with family and friends, finding the best brunch spots, and taking quiet walks by the ocean.

Instagram: www.instagram.com/hafsakamara
Facebook: www.facebook.com/KamaraHafsa
Website: www.hafsakamara.com
Photo by: Hannah Lorsch - www.instagram.com/ hannahlorschphotofilm/

The Four Silver YaYa's

By Alicia Bravo

Courage

"What lies behind us and what lies before us are tiny matters compared to what lies within us."

~ Ralph Waldo Emerson

Chapter 1

The Four Silver YaYa's

By Alicia Bravo

I was young, in my twenties, married with two children, and the manager/hairstylist of a hair salon in an upscale department store. The salon was very busy one day when a five-foot, feisty, silver-haired lady in her mid-seventies walked in for a haircut. She was very sure of herself and knew what she wanted. We didn't hit it off very well as she demanded that I cut her hair in a way I disagreed with.

After that struggle with the haircut/style, she returned in a month and loved the haircut so much, she said, "Now, that was the best haircut ever!" Being of Jewish descent, she said, "I'm sending you all my friends – three of them that I trust and play mahjong with every week." I won stylist of the year with those four wise Jewish yayas, all silver-haired, spirited ladies in their seventies. They cared about me, especially Raye. I had won her over through intimate, juicy conversations about her life.

Raye was exciting with stories about being a mother, being widowed in her forties with four children, and running her deceased husband's business. She found strength for herself and her children. She ran that business and became very successful, empowered, and stronger than ever. This was a time when women-owned businesses were unheard of.

Hazel was a friend of Raye's who was punctual, petite, silver-haired, and also in her seventies. She was a widow who had raised four sons. More soft-spoken than Raye, Hazel wasn't much interested in men. Her ex-husband was a sex addict, so she was turned off by men. She loved the arts and reading, as well as being a docent at a museum. She loved playing cards, mahjong, with weekly ladies' lunches at her house. Hazel coached me on manners, pronunciation, and what to say around men. Her lady-like advice was, "Don't give it all away. Create some mystery about yourself that keeps them guessing. Be smarter than they are and one step ahead. Keep some things for yourself, and don't sacrifice yourself trying to please them all the time."

Then there was Gertrude, who was outspoken and even more cynical about men. She had a bitter divorce but was happy to be alone and nesting in her small condo with a life full of activities. "Who needs men anyway?" was her motto. However, she was very supportive, overweight, wore her big hair with a big personality, and was quite outspoken on topics that you shouldn't get started on because she would have the last word. "Just don't play into men's games, and don't give in. Stand your ground and be empowered for what you believe in." Accountability was her motto. She had an accounting business before she retired.

Next was Mary, the detective. She had an innate sense about men that was quite accurate. "See what he's up to… find out, don't let him know that you know, and gather all the facts before presenting them. Make sure they're true." Mary was a gatherer of facts. He wasn't going to get away with anything. Mary was always suspicious, even when there wasn't anything to suspect. She could easily spot a liar. Radar Mary.

My marriage at that time was in shambles. Little did I know that in several years, I would find myself divorced, with two girls, and strapped financially before I was even 30 years old.

Raye really cared about me and could tell I was troubled. She began to coach me and help empower me. She listened and encouraged me to be strong and courageous. Her friends banded together and also supported me by sending more clients and buying more services. Raye told me how she was married four times, and that love is just around the corner when you least expect it. She had lovers she kept secret from her children. She told me about all the steamy dates she had and what a desirable woman she was – so irresistible to men. She told me that once she went on a weekend date with a man and he got a hotel room. She said, "Can you believe that son-of-a-bitch tried to lay me on the first date?" I asked her if she slept with him, and she said, "On the second date." Consensual, of course, with all her steamy love affairs.

At 80 years old, Raye slapped the salon owner's butt and told him, "If I were 20 years younger, I would have you." That's how confident she was with men. She told me, "You're young, beautiful, and you'll find a good husband again. I'm sure of it." Her advice was, "Don't sleep with them unless you want to. They'll try like hell, but don't do it. Wait until you find them irresistible."

Raye had this mink stole her first husband had given her as a gift. He told her how beautiful she was and that every time she wore it, he would marry her all over again. Raye said the mink jacket was charmed. She met all four husbands whenever she wore that jacket. She met her second husband wearing that jacket, and the marriage lasted four years. She divorced that son-of-a-bitch. She met the third husband wearing that jacket, but he passed away from a heart attack (like the first husband). The fourth husband was the love of her life. She loved and cherished him, but cancer took him. Moving on, Raye met the fifth suitor but kept him as a boyfriend. She wore that mink jacket the night she met him, too!

At 80 years old, marriage just wasn't in the stars, but sex was still very much part of her life. Who knew? I did, and I heard all about it!

Raye gave me that jacket because she didn't need it anymore. She knew I was divorced and single. She told me to wear it to a special occasion, and I would be sure to meet my husband that night. I had a good friend whose hair I cut, Jay, and he was going to his work's Christmas party at the Wrigley Mansion the following Saturday night. He had just broken up with his girlfriend. So, he asked me if I was available that night. I was, so I went with him. I asked if his ex-girlfriend would be there, and he said, "Yes." So, I wore a busty, form-fitting, red velvet, seductive dress, put my hair up, and wore Raye's charmed jacket.

The jacket worked! I met my husband that night. Jay went to talk with his ex-girlfriend for two hours. So, this handsome blonde guy came over to meet me. It was a charmed evening, and I didn't even know his name! He left the party and, apparently, I made quite the impression on him. He worked with Jay and asked Jay if it would be okay to contact me. Jay said, "Yes." When I got to work the following week, I had flowers and a card asking me to dinner. Of course, I said YES to dinner! It was magical. We dated for one and a half years and then got married. The rest is history. We've been married for 23 years!

Alicia Bravo

Alicia Bravo is an Arizona-based native of four generations living in the desert. She is a very passionate, intuitive hair salon owner and colorist/stylist. Since the beginning of her career, her first love was writing. This led to life experiences such as confessions and juicy secrets heard from behind the stylist's chair. The driving force that led to "I can't wait to hear the rest of the stories" of the silver yayas who came in resulted in her clients sharing their juicy secrets of wisdom, love, steamy love affairs, and other life dramas.

Alicia has had the opportunity of hearing this great wisdom from caring, loving women who are genuinely fond of this desert girl who grew up in the barrios of Phoenix, Arizona. Alicia is of Spanish and French descent, growing up speaking fluent Spanish with two hermanos (brothers) and three hermanas (sisters). Alicia is an accomplished hairstylist, entrepreneur, and salon owner. She really takes the time to get to know people, which opens up a wealth of information about what's inside each person. Being able to see people for who they truly are and listen closely to their stories represent her greatest gifts.

Contact information:
https://bravosalonaz.com/
https://www.linkedin.com/in/alicia-bravo-18942511/

The Last Gift

By Amy Sutherland

"In the middle of difficulty lies opportunity."

~ Albert Einstein

Chapter 2

The Last Gift

By Amy Sutherland

I had an epiphany as I quickly ran down the hallway of my mom's retirement home to get to the dining room before it closed. I felt like I was barely keeping it together and that all of the activities, emotions, and tasks I was juggling were thrown up in the air, and I was frantically trying to catch them all.

You see, I was taking care of my terminally ill mother while having a full-time job, managing my household, dealing with stressful family dynamics, gathering up the items I needed to bring home to close out the family estate, and going through all of my parents' remaining possessions. And then there were all of my emotions on losing my last parent while also trying to be as supportive as possible to my mom.

A little backstory before I get to my epiphany. I was always close to my parents, talking to them both almost every day. When my dad transitioned, my mom wanted to learn how to take care of all the items my dad managed in their 60 years together. So, I taught my mom what she needed to know, including creating a simple tool to empower her to understand exactly what she needed to do and when. I called it her "Monthly To-Do List." As we would work through the day-to-day challenges, I remember her continually asking me in amazement,

"How do you know how to do this?" I would stop and think back to when I might have learned that particular task or how I knew how to work through a problem. I realized that what I found to be a normal part of my day was the accumulation of my experiences, which then developed me into who I had become.

You see, I have had many different jobs working with senior-level executives as an Executive Assistant, Office Manager, Process Manager, and Project Manager. Currently, I was a Project Manager in Corporate Strategy. I worked on diverse, intense, and complex projects with multiple departments and varying personalities. No project was ever the same, and most situations I was introduced to were things I had not been involved in before.

So, as I quickly ran down the hallway of my mom's retirement home frantically worrying about everything I was trying to manage, my epiphany came to me in that moment of chaos… that every job and every experience I had prepared me for that moment. That moment of supporting and loving my last parent, dealing with the responsibility of finalizing the family estate, and dealing with stressful family dynamics. All of those jobs – those experiences, workplace dynamics, and intense situations – had prepared me, trained me, and built up my stamina for what I was going through in that current situation. All of these thoughts flashed through my head, building one on top of another until I found my breath. It happened in seconds, and it was so revealing, so clear.

Having this new awareness gave me the extra strength to continue to move forward. It helped me realize and proved to me that we are never given more than we can handle, and every experience brings new learnings, a wisdom we can use. It gives us the tools to support us for the next steps in our life's journey.

And as I worked through closing out the wonderful lives my parents had built and fully lived, finalizing paperwork, and dealing with my loss, I often wondered… How do people handle this process who don't have the experiences or skillsets that I possess? You see, I was prepared for what happened, and it was still difficult to go through.

It was then that I realized it was all the emotions I was experiencing simultaneously – the loss of my parents I was so close to, the stress of family dynamics, and trying to manage my own life. Juggling those emotions was the most difficult. It felt like I was alone in the dark, in the middle of the ocean, with a lot of wet heavy clothes weighing me down with no land in sight. I was just trying to keep my head above water. The Trust, my parents documenting their wishes, my documentation of their personal and financial information… all these were the life raft pulling me toward the safety of the shore.

When you are so emotional and in a stressful state, it is harder to make good decisions. Having a roadmap to follow helped me handle everything per my parents' wishes, as well as understand what they had, where it was located, and what to do. I didn't have the extra stress of worrying about what my parents had intended without legally documenting it, missing accounts, where the insurance policy was, or not having the password to the family computer.

Soon before my mom transitioned, we were in her bedroom, and she looked at me and said, "I am so sorry you have to go through this." Even then, my mom was looking to support me. What we both didn't see during that moment was how valuable my parents' wisdom was in preparing their estate plans, as well as working with me, so I understood their personal and financial information. That knowledge helped support me through the time of losing both of them. I feel it truly was the last gift my parents ever gave me.

So, as I healed and began the next chapter of my life, I thought… How can I help people prepare their loved ones for the inevitable? How can I empower them and their loved ones so they can have clarity and peace of mind? How can I shift the feeling of discomfort about talking and planning about your end of life into an opportunity to love, support, and take care of your loved ones up until the very end?

And so, an idea started to bubble to the surface of my mind. I decided to create a place where I could share my experiences and knowledge – my wisdom with everyone who might be overwhelmed or unsure of where to start. This idea developed into My Coach Amy.

I started by creating complementary support tools to assist everyone with organizing and documenting their personal and financial information. I also created coaching and consulting sessions. Coaching sessions for people wanting extra accountability, guidance, and support, while they are organizing and documenting their own personal and financial information. Consulting sessions for people who want their personal and financial information organized and documented for them.

Your estate planning determines who is in charge of your estate and fulfills your wishes. My Coach Amy was created to complement this planning with organizing and documenting what you have, where it is, and what to do.

My hope is that my life experiences and knowledge can empower you and that the tools I have created can help you determine the best way to provide support, clarity, and peace of mind to your loved ones. That this can be the last gift you provide your loved ones just as my parents provided me.

Amy Sutherland

Amy Sutherland was born and raised in the Midwest. After losing both parents in the span of two and a half years, Amy decided to create a new life adventure and move to Arizona. After finalizing her parents' estates, Amy realized the importance of sharing the information she learned. Amy created My Coach Amy as a way to provide support, clarity, and peace of mind for people wanting to prepare their loved ones to handle their affairs.

Amy has over 25+ years of corporate experience working with senior-level executives, most recently as a Project Manager in Corporate Strategy.

Her combined background in problem-solving, organizational skills, relationship building, project management, and coaching expertise makes her uniquely qualified to guide and support people through the process of organizing and documenting their personal and financial information.

Amy loves to travel and hike but is especially passionate about animals. She served as a Volunteer Adoption Counselor with PAWS in Chicago for several years. She has fostered cats and dogs and currently has a cat that behaves like a dog.

Estate Trustee / Administrator
Certified Project Management Professional (PMP)
Certified Empowerment Coach and Energy Leadership, Life and Corporate Coaching (iPEC)

Contact info:
https://www.mycoachamy.com/
https://www.facebook.com/mycoachamyllc
https://www.linkedin.com/in/sutherlandamy/

Scan Me!

The Box

By Andrea Brundage

There is a voice that doesn't use words. Listen.

~ Rumi

Chapter 3

The Box

By Andrea Brundage

The box was tucked away in the top of the closet. It belonged to my mom, and I knew the things inside were precious to her. Placing it carefully on my parents' bed, I would remove the lid to reveal the treasures. The contents belonged to my grandmother, a woman my mom barely knew, and a woman I longed to know.

ॐ ॐ ॐ

On October 1, 1925, my mother was born to Andrew and Ethel. She was their first child and was born premature and weak. Considering the times, her chances of survival were slim. She was named Colleen, a most fitting name for this tiny Irish girl.

According to my mom, her mother gave her heavy cream for additional fat and nourishment. She believed that rich cream and her mother's love were the reasons she survived. Is it any wonder my mom always enjoyed a glass of milk with her meals?

In 1926, Jack was born. *Jackie* was the apple of my mom's eye. She adored and protected her baby brother, always. He grew into a handsome man, and in the box were photographs of him. My favorite was him in a white military uniform, a twinkle in his eye, and a smile on his face.

❧ ❧ ❧

There are sketches, mostly of women, some embellished with water-colors. They have bobbed hair with soft waves, some wear fancy hats, and all are glamorous.

Grandmother was talented.

❧ ❧ ❧

There is a tan leather box with small glass windows. On top, a dial with a directional arrow. The words *Use Film No 116* are printed on a metal ring underneath the dial. Opening the back cover reveals the words *No. 2A Brownie, Model C.*

A scored, metal lever is on top of the box and when slid in either direction, makes a sound that pleases me.

Click, click, click.

Grandmother took photographs.

❧ ❧ ❧

There is a round sepia-colored tintype wrapped in tissue paper. The beautiful baby had a round face, inquisitive eyes, and brown hair. Mom said, *"This is my baby sister, Roberta. She died when she was eight months old."*

Grandmother lost an infant.

❧ ❧ ❧

The word *Photographs* is embossed on the front. Glued prominently on the inside cover, a quote cut into the shape of a heart. It reads, *To Love and Be Loved is Every Woman's Right.*

Grandmother was ahead of her time.

The carefully placed photos are mounted on the black pages. The album is neatly tied on one side and the bow is still intact.

Grandmother was intentional.

ॐ ॐ ॐ

My grandmother is wearing a silky robe over printed pajama bottoms and shiny black ballet-style slip-ons. Thick dark hair, dark sparkling eyes, full lips, and that beautiful smile. Grandpa is dressed in a white button-down shirt, neatly tucked into his slacks. His belt, like his shoes, look to be of brown leather. His thick dark hair, that grin, those sparkling eyes. In the photo, they are standing side-by-side, arms around one another's waists. The next photo, he's seated on a rocking chair, and she's playfully draped across his lap. Posing for the camera, all smiles.

Click, click, click.

Young love, captured moments, uncertain futures.

ॐ ॐ ॐ

There is a blue notepad, *GOLD METAL Note Book No. 37* printed on the front cover.

The first entry reads, *August 1st, 1929, 97 lbs.*

Inside the front cover are hand-written notes, a sketch of a woman, and in perfect cursive, *Mrs. Andrew (Ethel) Cleaver, age 20.* And then page after page of dates, columns, numbers. What does this mean?

Grandmother was young and she was keeping track of something.

ॐ ॐ ॐ

The inside back cover contains another sketch of a woman, along with the names *Colleen, Jack,* and *Roberta.* Her children, their birthdates, and delivery times noted.

There is a page with the words *Books I've Read* written in the top margin. The numbered list covers several pages: *Kathleen Norris, Ernest Hemingway, Booth Tarkington, Sinclair Lewis, Will Rogers*, and others.

The last entry: #152 - The Rainbow Trail, Zane Grey.

Grandmother loved to read.

 They are sitting next to each other on a bed, smiling. My grandmother dressed in a floral sleeveless jumpsuit and wearing dainty slippers embellished with feathers. She has a thin string of white pearls around her neck. So feminine, so beautiful.

My mom's about four years old and is wearing a light-colored dress, matching sweater, thick stockings, and black Mary Janes. Her hair is thick, dark, and her soft bangs frame her eyes. Her mother's arm is gently wrapped around her. They look happy. But wait, is that a hospital bed?

Click, click, click.

Grandmother smiled. They smiled.

The sanatorium. Kearney, Nebraska. Tuberculosis unit. 185 miles from home.

The dates, columns, numbers carefully written in the blue notepad, I now recognize as her vital signs. Her temperature and weight were taken twice a day, and she was documenting her journey. There are notations about color (blood) and procedures. There are names of visitors like *Cody* (her nickname for my mom), and *George* (her brother*)*, and many others.

Grandmother was dying.

❧ ❧ ❧

The last entry, August 21, Fri, 1931, 98.^{6}, 110.

On August 22, 1931, my grandmother died. My grandfather lost his beloved wife, and the children lost their mother. He was a widower with two youngsters to raise and a promise to fulfill. A promise to his dying wife that Colleen and Jack would never be separated.

Grandmother was gone.

❧ ❧ ❧

My mom recounted the car ride home after her mother died. It was just the two of them, my mom and her father. She said to him, "Daddy, where's my momma?" As an adult, she reflected, "That had to be the longest ride home for my Daddy."

❧ ❧ ❧

There is a white satin ribbon. The letters M-O-T-H-E-R glued to one side. There are some dried flowers - mostly broken into little pieces now. A sign of days gone by.

My mom tells the story of her brother, *Jackie,* standing on his tip-toes peering into their mother's casket. She reflects, "I remember that so clearly. It's sad he was too young to remember her."

❧ ❧ ❧

The children were raised together and remained close throughout their lives.

Promises kept.

❧ ❧ ❧

The Box offers glimpses into the life of a beautiful woman, my grand-mother. The contents illustrate one who loved deeply, laughed often, and adored her children. What a gift she left behind.

The pearl necklace, the handwritten notes, inspiring quotes, funny poems, words of wisdom, and sketches. The carefully curated *Photographs* album that contains pages and pages of smiles – her smiles, his smiles, their smiles. Proof of a happy and loving family.

Grandmother left a loving legacy.

My mom passed away on December 13, 2020. She lived a full 95-years, and her legacy lives on through her children, grandchildren, and great-grandchildren.

Like her own mother, my mom loved deeply.
Mom displayed acceptance and grace.
Mom laughed often, cried some, consoled, counseled, and served others.
Mom exemplified love.
Mom encouraged us to accept others just as they are.
Mom left a loving legacy.

After all, she was her mother's daughter.

I now have *The Box*. It is tucked away in the top of my closet.

Andrea Brundage

Andrea Brundage is a Professional Organizer and Bringer of Calm. Andrea says, "Helping clients create supportive spaces is my gift and my passion." Andrea's been organizing and streamlining homes and corporate offices for 15+ years. As an expert organizer, published author, speaker, and workshop facilitator, she has appeared on numerous television programs, and her interviews and quotes are often found in notable publications. Turning chaos into calm is Andrea's superpower.

Andrea has authored two books:
SIMPLIFY: 8 Simple Principles to Turn Your Chaos into Calm and *The Organized Estate: A planning booklet*

www.AndreaBrundage.com
www.ProfessionalOrganizerAZ.com
(480) 382-1085

Scan Me!

The Divinity of Sisterhood

By Becky Norwood

"I felt like I was being carried over the threshold of loss.
Yet, I knew I was not walking alone…
because the women around me showed me
what healing looks like."

~ Anna White

Chapter 4

The Divinity of Sisterhood

By Becky Norwood

As a book publishing expert, I have had the privilege of working with a wide variety of authors.

Working with the authors of *Wisdom of the Silver Sisters* has filled my soul in a different, more profound way. It has been an experience I will forever treasure. My heart is filled with gratitude with each contributor, my mind exposed to a vast array of life experiences and unmatched wisdom. The diversity of expression has been impressive – the joy of connection and sisterhood filling my soul with calm and delight.

Having grown up in an atmosphere of abuse and isolation, I had no opportunity for friendships as a youth. Each time I was "caught" enjoying the beginnings of a friendship, it would be quickly snuffed out by a paranoid and controlling father. Every conversation I had with someone I formed a friendship with would require a recitation of each and every word that was spoken.

Even letters to my grandparents, aunts, uncles, and cousins were censored, always becoming a word-for-word dictation of what my father would allow to be shared. Each letter had to be read to him before it could be mailed.

As I grew into adulthood, I was a loner. Having friendships was something that didn't come naturally to me. I know it deeply affected my life. The richness of friendship eluded me simply due to a lack of self-confidence and feelings of unworthiness.

It has been through the process of putting pen to paper, even eventually writing my first book, *The Woman I Love* (that woman is me), that allowed my truest healing to begin.

Thankfully, my life now is infinitely different than those early beginnings.

The following is the essence of what I have gained from my sisters of the heart: authenticity, vulnerability, love, sage wisdom, laughter, life lessons, support, discovery, deep joy, and so much more.

No one can whistle a symphony. It takes a whole orchestra to play it.

The quote above holds true for our lives as well. We cannot be an island to ourselves and expect to thrive.

I will begin with Ingrid E. Ingrid is a spiritual life recovery coach. We met through a business networking meeting and immediately hit it off. Eventually, she published her bestselling book, *The Emotional Dictionary of the Soulful Self*, through my company. I also began sessions with her to work through excavating and uprooting deep wounds that continued to haunt me. In the process, our friendship has grown. Ingrid has a "sparkle plenty" personality, radiating joy and fun. Through our friendship, I have come to know of her past and the journey of healing that brought her where she is today. I still tend to be very serious, though her treasured weekly Monday evening dinner and games at my home have brought laughter, singing, conversation, crazy fun and, most of all, sparkle to my life. She graces everywhere she goes with her sparkle, wit, charm, and deep intuitive wisdom. Bonus: My family enjoys her, too!

Rev. Maggie M., who has also written a chapter in this book, brings me a friendship of profound wisdom and insights, an incredible sense for business, along with impeccable authenticity. We met some years ago at a Brendan Burchard event where I just happened to sit beside her on the first day of the first session of the event. With a packed auditorium, chairs so crammed together that no matter where you sat, you were literally "rubbing shoulders" on both sides, we struck an immediate friendship. Her business is called Brilliant Breakthroughs. Now, we're preparing to launch the fifth book in her series, *Brilliant Breakthroughs for the Small Business Owners*. We have laughed and cried together, through challenging health issues, through successes and "failures," and I always reflect on our rich and insightful conversations, days, weeks, and months after they have occurred. I know she always has my back, and I have hers. A phone call, Zoom meeting, or text message away, I know I can connect for a quick pick-me-up or a long conversation shedding light on her incredible business acumen, wisely guiding me to an entirely different outlook on business and life issues I face.

Sue F., a free-spirited soul, who grew up in the U.K. post-WWII, fearlessly traveling the world completely solo, is one of my earliest true soul sisters. After a forty-year career as a top-performing anesthesiologist, she retired to begin her "second act" at age 71 as an entrepreneur with her business called *"Wisdom to Wealth Mastery."* A skilled videographer, her passion for life, healthy, active lifestyle, connection to her family and clients keeps her mind and body active. Our long, refreshing, and rich conversations are filled with pearls of wisdom, becoming a catalyst for my healing process. She wrote the foreword for my book and has long been my champion.

Betty C. is my fascinating divine sister whose professional career is leading oil and gas exploration teams in high-risk offshore deep-sea environments. She is currently in Israel, leading one of those teams. We met through an introduction by another soul sister who was publishing her book, *Your Emergence from Leadership to Heartship*. It also became a number one bestseller and is still topping the charts. Our every conversation is filled with her deeply intuitive guidance, along with raw and authentic sharing and brilliance.

Junie S. hails from the same city where Sue F. lives, in Victoria, B.C., and they've even met. Junie is a book writing coach whom I deeply admire. Upon meeting, we heart-connected immediately. Junie is an accomplished author of several books, including, *Your Life Matters – 8 Simple Steps to Writing Your Story*, *Re-Write Your Life*, and several fun journals and coloring books. Currently, she's writing a fantastic book entitled, *Re-Write to Re-Ignite Your Life*. By trade, she's a psychotherapist who has married her skills with the power of the pen, teaching many to discover healing and, ultimately, sharing the wisdom that comes from self-discovery. You will read her touching chapter in the pages of this book.

Traci K. and her family love entertaining and, indeed, my husband and I have enjoyed many meals around their dinner table surrounded by a diverse array of friends. Having never had children of her own, Traci met and married her second husband after recovering from the loss of her first husband in a car accident. Reid has two children, whom Traci welcomed with open arms, calling them her "bonus children." Smart, witty, a fabulous cook, we always pick up where we last left off, whether it is weeks, months, or years since we last spoke.

I wish I could continue showcasing more of my incredible soul sisters. Sisters like you – sisters like Sandy and Sharyn who are the inspiration behind this book you are reading. Space does not allow me to do so.

My divine sisters come in many different flavors, mindsets, backgrounds, and views on life. Each has blessed me and spurred me to become the best me I can be. In the process, I have learned to reciprocate the joy and support of sisterhood.

We each need and deserve the richness of divine sisterhood. That is the purpose of *Wisdom of the Silver Sisters*.

Becky Norwood

#1 International Bestselling author, speaker, & book publishing expert, **Becky Norwood** is CEO of *Spotlight Publishing™*. Widely recognized for the empowering and intuitive way she guides others to weave storytelling into their books and marketing. She incorporates her methods with sound marketing that is the pathway for business expansion and audience growth.

Becky has brought over 300 authors to #1 bestseller. Through her Author Studio TV Show, countless listeners have heard her interviews of both authors and experts offering sage advice. She offers an extensive catalog of services supporting emerging and established authors.

Becky believes that a well-told story is a gateway for growth, sharing, and a way to unite humanity. She is an advocate for the positive that comes from sharing our creative genius and impacting our world in positive ways.

Website: https://SpotlightPublishing.Pro
Email: becky@spotlightpublishing.pro
Facebook: https://www.facebook.com/
      SpotlightBookPublishing
LinkedIn: https://www.linkedin.com/in/
      beckybnorwood/

Scan Me!

Investing in the Stuff of Memories

By Betsy Brill

Ntafendaka ntando la mpos'e'ola!
"One does not cross a river by merely longing for home."

~ Congolese Proverb

Chapter 5

Investing in the Stuff of Memories

By Betsy Brill

When I was in my early 40s, I was with a group of women friends when one of them brought up investing. Another stopped the discussion, lamenting that she had spent all of an unexpected inheritance on a fancy sports car, and that talking about money was just too painful for her! Seriously! She was out of work at the time, living with a friend, and couldn't bear to discuss money.

Why are finances taboo for so many? My parents NEVER discussed money in front of me. I married at 20, and my husband handled everything. I was a thrifty young wife without a full understanding of the big picture.

Very unwise.

When we divorced after ten years, I left with a small cash settlement that I put into a savings account while figuring out my new life as a single mom. I also took out a credit card in my own name—a big deal at the time.

I was outrageously lucky a few months later to be hired to edit a book on personal finance.

While correcting grammatical errors and rearranging sentences, I wised up. I learned about the usurious interest rates on that new credit card and realized I could "save" 18 percent a year by paying off my purchases monthly. I learned about paying myself first by investing a bit of every paycheck before spending the rest.

I learned about no-load (commission-free) mutual funds and retirement planning. I invested part of my modest settlement in mutual funds at Fidelity and opened an IRA. I continued to invest the maximum in an IRA every year.

And I swore I would never let myself be clueless about money again.

When I got together with my second husband, a university professor, I made sure he was fully invested in his school's retirement plan and IRAs. We maxed out our retirement savings with automatic investments – and budgeted our lives on what remained.

Talking about money is important, even if it feels painful. My friend's exhilaration at driving her sexy little car had long been lost to despair. STUFF (including snazzy cars) will not pay the rent when a job disappears.

It's so tempting to splurge with "found" money like an inheritance, a bonus, a prize, part-time income, etc. Might investing half of her windfall before spending the rest have kept my friend afloat during her rough times?

Though not the book I edited, *"Financial Planning for Dummies,"* by Eric Tyson, is a brilliant guide to personal finance. I highly recommend it.

As a risk-averse university professor and a freelance writer/designer, my husband and I are not ultra-wealthy due to what we learned from that book. No designer clothes, no mansion filled with expensive STUFF. None of the four cars we owned over 40 years was the kind that commercials tell us we "deserve."

But we are financially flexible, comfortable in retirement, and often surprised by the size of our nest egg. AND we have been apparent jet-setters from the get-go.

We have stood in the shadow of the Sphinx, marveled at the glory of Rome, ascended the Eiffel Tower, touched the remains of the Berlin

Wall, and (admittedly not on everyone's bucket list) traveled in a dug-out canoe on the Congo River.

People often decide late in life to travel – only to find that their bodies can no longer keep up. With my hip aching as I write this, I am so glad we were wise enough to bump through Asia on busses and trek on foot in Nepal when we were younger!

We did many things to scratch our travel itch while rigorously saving for retirement – foremost among them, not spending money on expensive STUFF we felt compelled to protect by staying home.

Housing eats up most people's monthly budget. Covering that basic cost creates "found" money for travel.

We started with home exchanges (www.homeexchange.com), including one in which we stayed in a Parisian's apartment while he and his family lived in our San Francisco cottage. An Italian family squeezed into our little house while we wandered about their 2-level penthouse before walking to the Duomo and exploring Milan every day. We fell in love with Provence during home exchange(s) there.

For maximum flexibility, we began letting other people pay our mortgage by renting out our furnished home, STUFF and all when we were away for the longer periods. Renting our home during a 2001 sabbatical allowed us to apply what we would have paid in rent that year to buy a village house in Provence. And, yes, we rent that out to cover expenses. Let me put it this way: Other people pay to sleep in my bed – when I'm not in it!

"But what about your STUFF?" people cry. "Aren't you worried about your STUFF?"

I always respond, "Well, we don't own expensive STUFF. And no amount of STUFF is as precious as our memories of that journey on an elephant in Thailand, the camel trek in India, the temple ceremonies in Bali...

We were helping a friend move things into a storage unit a few years ago. A cheerful sign in the company's office shouted, "Your STUFF deserves more space."

I've known people who paid to store their STUFF for so many years that by the time they unloaded their units, they had forgotten what was inside. They had paid to store STUFF instead of paying themselves with monthly investments. And most of that forgotten STUFF wound up being discarded years later!

When I think of that monthly payment, I see a camel market in Egypt, the Great Wall of China… a comfortable retirement that allows yet more travel.

Aside from home exchanges or renting our home while traveling, we always "found" money for travel by using airline credit cards.

We charge our daily expenses to frequent flyer credit cards – BUT, thanks to my early lesson in personal finance, we live within our means and pay those high-interest cards IN FULL every month. Not buying random STUFF helps.

We treat our cards like a checking account that we can't overdraw. Paying for normal expenses like clothing, groceries, gasoline, restaurants, theatre, etc., pays for our future travel at the same time (interest-free, at that).

Credit card miles have transported us to home exchanges in Paris, Provence, New York, Amsterdam, Milan, Bali, and more. And remember, no money changes hands when you live in someone else's home while they live in yours. Free housing. Free plane fare.

Frequent flyer miles aren't as flexible as paid tickets. There often are limitations on when you can travel, etc., but the world opened to us when we overcame the hassle and figured out how to fly for free.

I share common wisdom with others my age: We accumulate STUFF when we are younger, and we anxiously unload the very same STUFF as we grow older.

Adventures don't fade away, jammed into storage units and forgotten. They are priceless treasures that really do last as long as our memories do.

Betsy Brill

Betsy Brill is a woman of a certain age… among the first to be vaccinated against polio in the 1950s, and among the most eager to receive the COVID19 vaccine in 2021. She's a former journalist, editor, and publication designer.

She worked for the *Houston Post* as a photographer; taught journalism at Stephens College in Columbia, Missouri; was editor and art director of *San Francisco* Business magazine; and went on to work as a freelance editor and designer for Apple, Levi's, and others. She has edited and designed six editions of her husband, Ken Kobre's, textbook,

Photojournalism: The Professionals' Approach.

In 1996, she and Ken, a photojournalist and professor of photojournalism, traveled for nearly a year through Egypt, India, Bangladesh, and Indonesia to collaborate on "The Power of Small Change," an in-depth exploration of microfinance approaches in those countries. Published as a 5-part series in the original *San Francisco Examiner*, the project was nominated for a Pulitzer Prize.

With two dear women friends, Betsy is a co-founder of HandUp Congo, a small non-profit that finds partners for projects aiding women in the remote village of Lotumbe in the Democratic Republic of Congo. (In Lotumbe, she is called Mama Bombambula.)

In 2020, Betsy abandoned her computer for clay and enthusiastically embraced sculpting and hand-building pottery. She lives in San Francisco, southern France, and sometimes in Scottsdale, Arizona, where her daughter resides.

She colors her hair, or it would be silver.

www.handupcongo.org
www.facebook.com/betsybrill
www.ourplaceinprovence.com
Betsyb123@mac.com
PO Box 15306, San Francisco, CA 94115

Scan Me!

Meditation Saves My Life

By Bonnie Barnard

Instead of telling God about your big problems,
tell your problems about your big God.

~ Rev. Michael B. Beckwith

Chapter 6

Meditation Saves My Life

By Rev. Bonnie Barnard

I am allergic to bee stings.

I am allergic to a lot of things, but any kind of insect bite is the worst. When I was six years old, my family went on a summer week-end get-away, renting a cabin in the woods with a lake on the property. The air was thick with clouds of mosquitos. We were covered in a stinky repellent. It didn't stop the mosquitos from deciding that I was their next prime rib dinner, and the family trip was over. My body was covered with so many mosquito bites, all swollen pink, millions of times the size of the original bite. My eyes swelled shut, I had difficulty breathing, and my parents decided it best to get me home and seek medical care.

Bee stings are worst. I am one of those people who can die once stung. Mosquitos are like baby vampires, stinging to withdraw blood as a food source. Bees are like attacking bears or rattlesnakes, stinging because they feel threatened. I don't know I buy this, but, for now, it is scientists' best explanation of these small-winged predators, burying a sack of venom under someone's skin. Terrifying really when your very life comes into play against such wee beings.

Twenty-five years ago, I flew to Kauai for a much-needed vacation. The reason I took this last-minute vacation was because it was almost free. A friend was going to lose his timeshare points, so I was given free accommodations. What a perfect opportunity, or so I thought at the time. I had some unexpected money come my way for airfare. I could rearrange work to front and backload my projects. I figured I would stay at the resort, avoiding a rental car so my trip would be virtually free. All the signs were there; I had to go. The Universe was gifting it to me after all.

The resort was across the street and down just a block from a Safeway. I walk to the store, loading up on groceries. I buy the makings for a hamburger dinner. Back at the condo, I thank the Great Spirit for all of the good It brings me. I take in the warm outdoor air lightly fragranced by plumeria blossom, mentally marking this moment in the mental file folder marked Heaven. I prepare a seasoned hand-pressed patty then bring it to one of several grills on the property to cook. Once done, I put it on a plate to walk barefoot back to my unit. Might I say, feet in the grass feels heavenly contrasted to boots in the rain I experienced merely hours before in Seattle. Until… yes, until… I step on a bee.

In scientifically determined self-defense, it stings me. No cell phone, as the average person didn't have them yet. No car. No open office. And no 9-1-1 as the island didn't have that system. What to do? I thought fast. I angle my foot up as to not push the stinger in further and hobble back to my unit. Once inside, I sit down on the couch, remove the stinger and meditate. My rationale is if I keep my pulse steady, not panicking, the venom won't race to my heart on the energy of hyperventilating. Instead of getting emotionally worked up, I calm myself. I envision a tourniquet a few inches below the bite, containing the poison, as I see healthy cells flowing Mozartesque in and around my heart. With my mind, I contain the venom from spreading. The rest of me is as peaceful as a monk in the mountains. Fifteen minutes later there is no evidence of a sting, except a slightly heavy and awkward feeling in my foot.

I am stung two more times. These times without provocation. Several years after Kauai, I was floating in a swimming pool outside of Tucson, Arizona, on another vacation. It was summer, so it was too hot to be outside unless immersed in a pool. I had a book in hand while floating on a netted mattress floaty when I see a bright orange wasp land in the pool for a drink, then take off to fly toward me, landing on my left upper arm opposite my heart. This was no self-defense; this was aggressive warfare. Upon landing, this beautiful orange-winged creature called Tarantula Hawk is the most painful of all insect stings in the United States. Once violated, I repeated my Kauai ritual meditating myself into well-being. Keeping the venom separate from the heart, while calming my body down.

A few months ago, I was stung, while tequila tasting at the Osuna tequila factory, a few miles outside of Mazatlán, Mexico. This time the location was my left pinky finger. Same routine --only standing up in the middle of a group – going deep within to calm, quiet, and contain. The tour guide pulled out the stinger. A military man insisted upon putting placing tobacco soaked in spit on the site to draw out the venom. This is the practice done while in battle. His wife said, "good thing you aren't allergic to bee stings," to which I smiled.

I thought, as you probably are, that maybe I had outgrown this allergy which would provide a logical explanation. Not so. When I was allergy tested recently, I am at the level of guaranteed death.

Meditation is a super-power. Prayer is its sidekick. These two practices have kept me and many others I work with healthy, empowered, steady, and, most importantly, alive.

Bonnie Barnard

Bonnie Barnard had her first direct experience of God at age five when she was praying over and singing to her vegetable garden. "A blanket of Divine Love wrapped me so fully that I vowed I would become a minister," Barnard says.

She has kept her commitment to that promise. Today she serves as a Spiritual Advisor supporting individuals in finding spiritual solutions to human problems and companioning individuals in maturing spiritually. This is done through individual sessions, online classes, and retreats. She is the author of five books, contributor to two, and hosts a blog on her website.

www.bonniebarnard.com

Scan Me!

The Overcoming of Incredible Odds

By Cat Parenti

*"Every leaf on every tree knows that
I love my Beloved."*

An Afghan Sufi Master

Chapter 7

The Overcoming of Incredible Odds

By Cat Parenti

My journey began in Brooklyn at age three, seeing visions of Afghanistan, the purplish-brown mountains, the ocher color plains, and the periwinkle sky. As I matured, I continued to follow my heart and visions, leading me to Afghanistan, where I met the man of my dreams. We had instant past life recognition of one another like an earthquake rippling through me, as planets collided, and suns died and were reborn. Jamal, an Afghan nobleman, an Islamic mystic, and I had a deeply passionate and loving relationship overlayed by the Soviet invasion, occupation, and the rise of the Afghan resistance. Jamal was a nobleman and a noble man.

We had a conscious conception on a ship in the ocean, and the dolphins followed us for five days. I knew our child would be a powerhouse. Finally, he was taken from me when the Soviets bombed Jalalabad with chemical warfare, and I was pregnant. With his dying breath, he asked me to promise that I would raise our child as a true Afghan. When I did, he passed, and I felt a strange sensation in my womb. Weeks later, he appeared to me in the Light Body and told me he passed his Sufi (Islamic mystical) lineage to our child.

The way of the Sufis is a humble, powerful, prayerful path strewn with miracles. The Muslims revere Jesus Christ, Moses, and Mohammed as great prophets and believe in the powers of Mother Mary, Angels, and other high adepts like my daughter Chandra to help mankind.

Miracle One was when I became ill with hepatitis A. The Afghan family I was living with decided to take me to a Sufi healer. We taxied to the old bazaar and walked the muddy rock-strewn lanes to a tiny adobe shop on an embankment. An old man with a white beard who sat on a carpet, listening as the Afghans talked. Then he took out a wooden scythe inlaid with brass and mother of pearl, recited from the Quran as he touched it to my forehead, lips, and chest. Next, he gave my family a tiny vial of rose oil and told them to put one drop in a glass of water to drink three times a day for three days, and I would be healed... and I was.

My daughter Chandra had a home birth with no drugs or surgeries, just an elderly naturopathic physician who had seen 3000 live births and snored through most of my five hours of labor. She awakened at appropriate moments to have my coaches give me certain herbal teas to assist me. Chandra was born wide awake, looking around, didn't cry, and breathed on her own after the umbilical cord stopped pulsing.

While we were resting together, Chandra took me on a journey out of the body. I was looking down on the cosmos. So many answers to many mysteries were given to me, and I kept mentally exclaiming in absolute wonder, "So that is why that happens!" Miracle Two

When Chandra was three months old, she was doing *mudras* (sacred symbols) with her fingers, like those of Jesus Christ, Christian, and Hindu saints.

At eight months, after giving her the recommended vaccinations, Chandra stopped all sound and movement. I was told she was a vegetable, and I should institutionalize her. Shocked, I refused to believe it!

I had a past life regression, whereby you are put in a light trance but aware of everything. A Native American male guide came through me, my voice dropped an octave. The woman conducting the regression asked him why Chandra came here disabled. The answer was, "The overcoming of incredible odds." Miracle Three. I began studying all alternative treatments to help Chandra.

At age two, she took the pen from my hand with her fist and placed it on a piece of paper. I steadied her fist, and she wrote 11 11. It wasn't until she reached age nine that a book by Solara called "*11:11*" on the sacred meaning of those numbers came out. Miracle Four.

After seven years of doing alternative therapies with Chandra, I felt safe enough to decide what I wanted to be when I grew up. Importing Afghan handicrafts to the States was out of the question. Instead, I realized that I had a wealth of knowledge on how to help people, abled or disabled. So I took certification courses and received a license in alternative therapies and opened my own practice Lymphatic Drainage, Afghan Aromatherapy, Metabolic Analysis, Color Therapy, and Chakra Balancing. I also began teaching these subjects in all the colleges in the Phoenix, Arizona area.

From age 11 to 15, Chandra attended the Gifted Children's Program at Arizona State University, studying Biology and Philosophy getting top marks. She always had a personal assistant since Chandra doesn't speak and only has gross motor usage of her hands. She communicated telepathically with her aides, and that is the way she runs her own business today. Miracle 5

Chandra wanted to study Quantum Physics, but it wasn't available then. After the ASU program shut down, she became bored, dropped out of high school at sixteen, and started her own "service to humanity" business. She does distance healing and creates tools, fractal videos through Quantum Physics and Sacred Geometry that make changes at the cellular level. Once when interviewed about different vibrational rates, the host asked what her vibrational rate was.

She replied, "One hundred million megahertz." The host said, "That is the Quantum Light Field." It is from there that she does her work.

Today, at age 38, she has overcome incredible odds. She is widely known as "Grandma" Chandra, a title given to her by Chief Golden Light Eagle of the Yankton Sioux. She does distance healing through her readings and by recommending her tools in Fractal Videos and essential oils that make changes at the cellular level. Following the Sufi Path of her father, Chandra brings compassion and mercy to people who suffer physically, mentally, emotionally, and spiritually. Miracle Six.

Testimonial:

"This highly intuitive being with a heart of gold can see, know, sense, and feel all that is necessary to guide us along our ascension process. When I saw Grandma Chandra, she sent rings of light pouring through my body, filtering out my inner fears allowing me to have the confidence and connection to higher knowledge needed to heal. She is vivacious, fun, and a truly ascended being of great knowledge and purpose. Her gentle and very powerful (way) allowed me to surrender to a heightened place with grace and ease. Grandma is a delight to be with." Gregory Joseph

Cat Parenti

A 2019 Amazon Gold Author for her sixth book, *Afghanistan: A Memoir from Brooklyn to Kabul*; Director Afghanistan Foundation – humanitarian aid work inside Afghanistan 1980-1990; Award – Intergovernmental Committee for Migration – helping Afghan refugees in Pakistani camps; Award – Hillary Rodham Clinton for Cat's books on and work in Afghanistan; Award – Division of Developmental Disabilities for work with the severely disabled; Award – 2016 Best Small Business in Mesa, Arizona, Grandma Chandra's LLC; Wholistic Practitioner: Certified Lymphologist, Afghan Aromatherapist, Color Therapist, Reflexologist, and Metabolic Counselor.

Today, at age 38, Chandra has overcome incredible odds. She is widely known as "Grandma" Chandra, a title given to her by Chief Golden Light Eagle of the Yankton Sioux. She does distance healing through her readings and recommends using her tools in Fractal Videos and essential oils that make changes at the cellular level.

Following the Sufi Path of her father, Chandra brings compassion and mercy to people who suffer physically, mentally, emotionally, and spiritually.

cat.parenti@gmail.com
https://www.catparenti.com/
https://www.grandmachandra.com/
520-508-0211 (Arizona Time)

Chandra Ahmed Khan

Chandra Ahmed Khan aka Grandma Chandra, despite severe physical limitations attended the Gifted Children's Program in Arizona State University between the ages of 11 and 15 while simultaneously attending high school. She excelled in biology and philosophy.

She started her own business serving humanity at age 16 which continues until the present. www.grandmachandra.com

A high intuitive, and an Ascended Master who reads Auras, Grandma Chandra heals people through the Light codes and frequencies within her Holographic Fractal videos, works in the Quantum Light Field with Sacred Geometric forms, high vibrational essential oils, Apps, and her healing green laser that are all personally encoded for each client.

Grandma's pre-birth contract was to come to Earth to help with Planetary Ascension. She is a multi-dimensional being who communicates through telepathy and distance healing with those around the globe who have Master Numbers in their birthdates. Like the Whales and Dolphins, she is clairvoyant, clairaudient, and clairsentient.

www.grandmachandra.com
https://www.facebook.com/grandmachandra11

Scan Me!

The Wrong Question

By Chelsea Sutton

"If I'd asked customers what they wanted,
they would have told me,
'A faster horse?'"

~ Henry Ford

Chapter 8

The Wrong Questions

By Chelsea Sutton

As my short pastel pink and purple curls fell into my eyes, I used one hand to move them and one hand to hold the microphone. Announcing the next three competitors, I sat in a swiveling black office chair at the top of an arena in Oklahoma City that held 10,944 people. There were another 15,000 people streaming online from across the globe. I was the first female in the history of Reining (a western horse sport, similar to a rodeo) to announce a NRHA major event.

How did I get here, you ask? This is a question I've been asking myself, too.

That's what I do well, you see; I ask questions.

At my ripe ol' age of 31, I count it all joy that I've been fortunate enough to:

Own three businesses

Have spent time in Europe & Asia

Won awards for community development

Have clients who run multi-million dollar brands and transform lives every day

Speak on stage to thousands of people
And any success I've had, I credit to asking questions.

Yes, you read that right. Asking questions.

Launching a marketing consultancy as a 21-year-old had unique challenges. Those who hire a consultant believe they've hired a crystal-ball reader, one who sees the future. As a 21 year old, I was barely figuring out what the future even was.

I learned that I didn't have to know everything - I just had to know the problem. The best way to guide someone's marketing is to first find out what part of marketing they're struggling with.

It's the chicken before the egg — the horse before the cart.

When I ask good questions, it affords me understanding.
With understanding, I can analyze.
By analyzing, I identify gaps.
Once I know what the gaps are, I can suggest bridges to those gaps.

As a young 20-something CEO, I hired staff and taught them my questioning philosophy.

Listen a lot.
Why are things down?
Discovery is what it's typically called.

This became our greatest tool.

Ask good questions → get good answers → to create good strategies. Repeat.

I began to apply this to other parts of my life — ehh — *every* part of my life.

Why isn't this social media post performing? Ask questions.
What was the graphic?
When was it posted?

Get to know a new employee better? Ask questions.
Where'd you grow up?
Why are you drawn to website development?

How to expand a successful product line? Ask the customer questions.
What do you enjoy about this product?
What problem were you dealing with before you found this?

AND THEN OUT OF NOWHERE
IT HAPPENED....

I uttered a thoughtful question to an industry leader. Without hesitation, he looked me dead in the eyes and said, "You're asking the wrong question!"

Now, before you say, "Chelsea, what's the big deal..." let me remind you - I ASK GOOD QUESTIONS.

I've been asking questions (intentionally) for 10+ years. *I get paid $150/hour to ask good questions.*

This specific question was about the judging system for Reining, the sport I was announcing the national event for. My father has spent the better part of 35 years developing the system. I've spent the better part of 15 years studying it.

My question was quite sophisticated {or so I thought}.

"This event is the best of the best - yet, judges have very different scores. What should we do to correct them?" I asked.

"That's the wrong question. It's not about the individual judges. The question is WHY are we commonly seeing the best of our judges make inaccurate calls?" This tenured official continued on to suggest that the issue is the environment: unclear standards for difficult scenarios, and working the judges for far too many hours.

That makes sense. Decision-making, focus, will-power: studies reveal these are depleting resources. With each decision, we deplete our reservoir. We saw this in the judging process.

MY NEXT QUESTION: Why hasn't this been fixed?

HIS RESPONSE, "Those in charge keep asking the same question you did. People focus on the wrong problem."

WOW. Talk about a shattered world view.

Not only was I enlightened on a new issue plaguing our sport, but now I wondered if I had been asking shallow or irrelevant questions all along.

Or, even worse...had I been solving the wrong problems all this time?

In some ways, the answer is yes.
The challenges that perpetually surfaced were exactly the ones I had been asking the wrong questions for.

Why didn't this one specific Facebook post perform?
Wrong question.

Instead, I should ask:
Am I increasing unique reach month-over-month?
Am I increasing sales via customer retention through Facebook content?

I want to grow my business - how do I increase revenue?
Wrong question.

Instead, I should ask:
How can I increase profit?
Is there internal waste to cut, in order to increase margin?

LESSON 1: It's not enough to ask good questions, we must ask the right questions.
After wallowing in my worry, nervous that everything I thought I knew about business had flown out the window, I remembered another lesson I had learned years ago:

LESSON 2: We must marry insight with inspiration.

It's not about seeking the answer from others, it's about seeking insight.

The path to success is plowed with the direction of your intuition.

This lesson helped me shift from being a student of business to being a strategist. A great problem-solver takes observation and aligns it with innovation to create a plan of action.

BAM — that was it.

It was aligning those lessons that led me to this moment, this seat - at the top of a 10,000 person arena with a microphone in my hand.

1. THE RIGHT QUESTIONS: I asked the producers what kind of event environment they wanted.
2. MY INSPIRATION: I observed the exhibitors. I watched spectators' responses to certain words and phrases. I watched other sports announcers. I dreamed. I asked myself how it could be different, better, more unique.
3. MARRYING those insights created exactly what Reining wanted. No one knew how to ask for it directly, but when it was offered - it was welcomed.
4. It was welcomed by the exhibitors, by the spectators, and by those who believed in me enough to hire me — the first female — to announce the second-largest Reining event in the entire world.

When asked about the iPhone, Steve Jobs said: "Some people say, 'Give the customers what they want.'" But that's not my approach.

Our job is to figure out what they're going to want before they do. I think Henry Ford once said, "If I'd asked customers what they wanted, they would have told me, 'A faster horse!' People don't know what they want until you show it to them."

Steve was right.

I thought it was all about being a problem solver. Now I know that is the wrong focus.

It's not about solving just any problem - it's about solving the right problem.

To do so, we must ask the right questions and dare to dream along the way.

Chelsea Sutton

Chelsea Sutton founded The Consult-Ment Agency, a marketing agency that provides consulting and management for marketing activities, after graduating top of her class in Entrepreneurship and Business Management from Arizona State in 2012.

Her love for capitalism, business structure & problem-solving brings a strategic business-driven approach to marketing. It's not just about what's trendy. It's about what works.

From startups to multi-million-dollar companies, The Consult-Ment Agency has managed accounts with 150k followers, achieved millions of impressions per year, and impacted revenue growth of over 20% increase per year.

Chelsea serves the next generation of business leaders as an Adjunct University Instructor for Social Media Marketing & Marketing Research!

Chelsea now runs three brands:
The ConsultMent Agency - A West-coast marketing agency
Visibiliti Creative - An East-coast marketing agency
ReinerStop - An online media company in horse sports

Originally from Buffalo, NY, she grew up on a horse farm in North Carolina (Go Pirates) and has been in Arizona since 2011. When not at her desk or out with a client, you can find her swing dancing, riding her horse, or traveling across the country behind a microphone, emceeing a horse show.

Chelsea is blessed to run ConsultMent & Visibiliti Creative with her high-school sweetheart of 15+ years, Travis. Now, operating as the CEO (Chief Espresso Obtainer) and lead strategist, her focus is on day-to-day operations, ensuring aligned client fit, and pushing strategists to be the best they can: for themselves, and for the clients ConsultMent serves.

CONTACT INFORMATION
Chelsea Sutton
Email: Chelsea@ConsultMent.Agency
Mail: 30020 N 60th Street, Cave Creek AZ 85331
Website: ConsultMent.Agency - VisibilitiCreative.com

SOCIAL:
Facebook: https://www.facebook.com/chelseajdSutton
Instagram: http://instagram.com/cimforgiven
LinkedIn: www.linkedin.com/in/chelseajdsutton

Scan Me

The Power of Color

By Cyndee Mubi

"Life Is About Using The Whole Box of Crayons"

~ RuPaul

Chapter 9

The Power of Color

By Cyndee Mubi

Color, what can we say, except to be grateful that we can see colors and the beauty they bring to us? However, some people don't even recognize colors, some people are repelled by colors, and some are less fortunate to be able to see colors, but for those who recognize colors in our world, do enjoy and appreciate what the Universe and Mother Earth give to us, with much love and gratitude. Did you know color travels faster than the speed of sound? Well, it does, and each color has its own vibration. Can you imagine the effects that can bring to oneself? These are just some of the reasons why I'm fascinated with colors, as are many others out there with the things they do, make and create that are absolutely amazing and beautiful.

I want to share a couple of experiences I've had using color with energy healing (Reiki). My first story to share, is when I was a vender at a Metaphysical Fair offering energy healing infused with color, this beautiful woman walked up and asked to have a healing session with my sacred colored silks. I had her lie down on the table and I started scanning her body to see if I could feel any areas that needed attention, and while doing so, I asked her if there were any areas she wanted to focus on. She said, "Just do your magic." So, I did.

I was very drawn to her heart area. I went to grab my pink sacred silk as it's for unconditional love, but not this time. This time I was guided to use my emerald-green sacred silk, which is one of the seven colors of the rainbow and one of the colors of the energy wheels or chakras that reside within us. I laid the green silk upon her chest, her Heart chakra and placed my hands up by her shoulders descending downwards so to send her the Divine, universal energies through my hands, through the green silk and into her body for healing. While doing so, an intuitive image came through, the only thing I could see was a male figure. At that very moment, I noticed the healing work I was a part of administering was very powerful and emotional, as I could see the tears cascading down the sides of her face.

The Divine energies and the green sacred silk were melding into her for some very deep healing. While she continued to lay there, I then covered her body with my white sacred silk, so all the healing that had taken place could settle within so she could rest in peace and tranquility for the remainder of the session. When the session was done, she was still pretty emotional, with tears running down her face. I asked her how she felt, she cleared her throat and started to share with me why she was very emotional. She told me her husband had unexpectedly passed away two months prior. I then realized why the green sacred silk was called upon. I gave her a big hug with some loving energies, and suggested she wear some green for a while.

My other healing experience was on this lovely lady, and she asked me to work on her droopy eye that was a result from cancer, but first I scanned her body for areas that could use some healing. I asked my higher self what color to use on her eye, as I would have chosen indigo for the Third-Eye chakra or purple for the Crown chakra, as those are two areas of the head or face that are the closest to her eye, but the color yellow is what I was hearing.

I was wondering why yellow, as that would be the color to use on the power center, also known as the "Solar Plexus" chakra. I didn't understand why I was guided to use that color on her eye, but

I eventually caved in and used that complementary color. I placed my yellow sacred silk all folded up on her eye, and within moments I could see this beautiful purple ray of light beaming out from under the silk. I was absolutely amazed to see such wonder. When the purple ray went away, I knew the healing was done. Wow, was it ever done! Her eye was no longer drooping. She walked out to the lobby where her husband was waiting for her, and he said, "Honey, your face, your eye, it looks normal again." He was so amazed at the healing that took place, as she and I were.

The powerfulness of color comes from the universe as a white light reflecting a spectrum of beauty. Blend it with the loving universal energies, and the two together will give you a life with much healing and joy. Color is a mid-point between pure light and pure darkness. Live, Laugh and Love in the "mid-point."

Cyndee Mubi

At a young age, I noticed a connection with colors and the effects they had on me. As a result, I became conscious about my clothing and accessories having to be color coordinated. In both middle and high school, I took classes that involved color, like art and Interior Design. Afterward, I attended an Academy for Fashion Merchandising, where I learned so much about colors in multiple ways. While finishing that, I was chosen out of the whole Academy to be taken under the wings of a local make-up artist who wanted to teach the new "Make-up Artist" about color pallets and make-up application.

Years later, when I had my spiritual awakening, I was hungry to learn about spirituality and related modalities like, energy healing (Reiki), and to this day, I continue to feed my soul. A couple of years later, it came to me to add color to the energy healing to enhance the healing process, so I personally looked into it, only to realize I didn't know how to blend the two, so I put that aside. A couple more years past, and it was brought back to my attention, but this time the stars were aligned. I did some research, and before I knew it, I was off to Switzerland to learn how to bring color and energy together for a beautiful and powerful vibrational healing experience.

You can reach me at:
Healingrays713@gmail.com
Cyndee Mubi at Facebook, Facebook Messenger, Instagram, and Eventbrite.

From Misfit to Mystic

By Dawn Katar

*"The invariable mark of wisdom is to see
the miraculous in the common."*

~ Ralph Waldo Emerson

Chapter 10

From Misfit to Mystic

By Dawn Katar

Now in my 8th decade of life, this time around, I often think of my grandma. What did I learn from her? What was her life ambition? What were her triumphs? Like many folks, I'm sure, I've had regrets of not asking more questions when I might have had the chance to do so. Some of my great memories of her were about her calm demeanor around chaos. I never saw her angry or short-tempered. She was the kind of woman who taught, *"If you don't have something nice to say about someone, don't say anything."* When she laughed, she laughed fully. She modeled this for my own mother, who seemed to struggle with being a worthy woman.

Now that I am looking through the eyes of a mother, I am astonished at how she managed to have a personal identity raising seven children. Oh, how I have often cried, "Mother, please forgive my ignorance." It's grand to have known two such resilient and loving women. What wisdom would I gather from knowing these amazing women?

I am now far more trusting and forgiving of my own foolish adventures as I consider the shy, insecure young girl I once thought I was. I looked at everyone around me and thought, "How is it I am with this family? I can try to understand them, but will they ever understand me?"

I know of many people who have felt that they did not fit in with the family that they lived with. Many have had experiences of trauma or denial of their identity. I am not unique because I grew up feeling like a misfit. This perception of life, 'not fitting in,' was a foundation for building my awareness of my mystical nature.

As I neared the event of receiving my first Holy Communion, I realized that my mystical nature was not common. I had often felt my guardian angel close to me, and Betty, as I called her, would seem to delight in getting me into trouble at school by sitting so close to me in my desk chair that I would fall on the floor. My first experience with my deep connection with Jesus was on the day of receiving the sacrament. Before the priest placed the Eucharist on my tongue, I experienced a brilliant ball of light shoot out from the tabernacle and enter my heart. My body was thrown back for a moment. Again, the nun's expression did not seem to convey understanding.

At other times, I had visits from Mother Mary so beautiful and so vivid that I was astonished that no one else seemed to see her. I am happy that when I told my mother about some of these visits, she didn't react with fear for my sanity, but she said, "That's really nice. Keep praying because you could be receiving a calling." I knew what that meant to her. I would possibly grow up to enter a convent, like a great aunt whom I was named after. I would explore that possibility several times over the years but knew I didn't seem to have the temperament for such a life. I became fascinated with reading about saints and felt a kinship with many of them. Except for the martyrdom thing that many were called to, I wanted to be a saint, not for the recognition as a saint but to live in the deep love of God that they seemed to have.

The calling, as my mother referred to it, was being revealed to me a little bit at a time. In high school, I sent away for information on several orders of nuns to look over and feel into the appropriate one. I admired these women, but it was not for me. In fact, when I lived alone and felt spiritually disconnected from my family, my church, and society at the 'ripe old age' of 21, I once again sent for information on some convents. I longed for spiritual community and had not really found what that meant. I had a huge laugh when I sat looking at the brochures for the convents and realized that there would be three vows, and I could only see myself staying true to two of the three. Poverty? Chastity? Check! Obedience? Seriously?

When that became crystal clear, I asked out loud, "What shall I do?" I then turned on my AM radio and found myself listening to an interview with a couple who were in town to share about connecting with your angels. I got chills and wrote down the information. It had been some years since I had my mystical experiences with Betty, Jesus, or Mother Mary. This all felt familiar, and so off I went to that lecture. At my private counseling session that followed, I heard Betty speaking to me again. Thrills and chills! Through the practice of connecting with my inner guidance daily, I found a deep spiritual connection – with my angels and a new spiritual community that grew across the country over time.

Just about three years later, as I walked along the Rock River in Illinois, I posed a question again. "What is my life purpose?" I shook when I heard a thundering voice answer. "You are to be a prophet of your age." Again, I thought, "Geesh! Don't prophets get killed, too?!"

Over the next few years, I continued working with my angel communication and asked to be guided to deeper states of consciousness. I received a small coaching push to trust myself to let go of the need to know and understand, which I practiced daily. Then one day, I found myself in a wonderful etheric place (like a super-lucid dream) and when I returned to the room that I was sitting in, my close friend and spiritual supporter excitedly told me about a visit from an entity that I had just channeled. My ability to work with my angels for protection and for clarity became a familiar skill that I might have had from other life spans. I found that I could 'leave' (the physical dimension) and have a conscious journey while Spirit shared messages of Wisdom through me. I discovered that I could also choose to place my awareness in an observation state and be witness to the Spirit sharing whenever I needed that experience.

Various tools, such as Breathwork, Past-life Regression, and focused therapies over many years would help me make peace with unresolved patterns. Continuing meditation and daily work with Spirit have become as important to me as drinking water. This is what I know now. Living a mystical life may look like a misfit life to those who have not touched that part of themselves yet. Living a mystical life doesn't mean isolation and disconnecting from pleasures, relationships, and adventures in learning. A mystical life brings joy and ease in choosing where the attention goes regarding every part of life. The biggie is knowing that I am not attached to making any of these choices to validate my existence or prove my worth. My mystical life is one of freedom!

Dawn Katar

Dawn Katar is a gifted channel for the Ascended Masters and a teacher of the Divine Principles. Her conscious connections with Spirit date to her earliest memories as a child. She calls herself an Open Channel of Divine Light because she has committed herself to receiving Light and wisdom from the highest possible realms in service to all who come with open hearts and minds.

As such, she has received and shared communication from many, many Ascended Masters, Angels, Extraterrestrial Beings of Light as well as Beings from the animal, plant and crystal kingdoms, including our Mother Earth, Gaia. Dawn Katar has been offering instruction, discourse and messages from the Ascended Masters publicly since 1971. She has assisted countless brothers and sisters of Light to open their own channel of communication with Spirit. She desires that everyone experience the personal guidance and love from their own team of angels and heavenly assistors.

Dawn Katar currently lives in Phoenix AZ with her beloved Twin Flame and husband, Darryl. They have two adopted and deeply loved children. Dawn's second passion is working with a non-profit organization that offers support and education to parents and caregivers with children who have mental/emotional challenges. She has helped develop programs from a peer-parent perspective to help guide parents to confident leadership for their own family and community to help transform child serving systems of care.

Email: openchannelresources@gmail.com
Phone: 602-690-7660
https://www.openchannelresources.com/

Scan Me!

Shame on Shame: SOS

By Deena Chester

"It is with Grace and Ease that feelings of shame can be released, and one's true self can flourish."

~ Deena Chester

Chapter 11

Shame on Shame: SOS

By Deena Chester, C.Ht

Is it possible that shame experienced in childhood can lead to a lifetime of mistrust, fear, withdrawal, perfectionism, control, self-doubt, blame, and disempowerment? Yes, and if you have found your way to this chapter, you have most likely experienced shame-the invisible enemy.

It was only in my late 40's that I had knowledge of the influence of shame and how it had impacted my entire life. The memories, like movie trailers, popped into my mind. At this point in my life, I know to pause, breathe, and offer gratitude to each memory. Without those journeys, I would not be who I am today and would not own a healing holistic business. I will be forever grateful to the clients and my husband that shared similar journeys. As they allowed healing, I continued to heal. I trust you can do the same.

As you read the examples below, allow yourself to remember your own experiences.

Shame-parent's discipline.
I was a quiet introverted child and feared my mother's wrath. I was well into adulthood before I realized that she was mentally unstable. When a family is dysfunctional, a child often thinks that is the norm.

I can still hear the sharpness in my mother's voice as she yelled at me for laughing to loud, "Deena if you don't behave, I will pull your pants down in this store in front of everyone and whip you." She made sure to say it loud enough that others could hear.

As I share this memory, I want to thank you for honoring this space with me. I was so embarrassed because she attracted the attention of those people. How could she do this? She drove home her favorite control statement, "What will people say?" What did I do wrong? Her actions and words were shaming. I was reminded that I shouldn't laugh or smile. I told myself that I must learn to be quiet and suppress my emotions and voice.

Shame-choices being scrutinized.

It was so exciting in the fall to go shopping for new school clothes, but it always had the same negative outcome. Mother would say "Deena, go pick out your one pair of school shoes and a few outfits." My little hippie rebel soul would find some clothes and usually boots.

I would exclaim, "Look what I found!" And the doom would begin. In her condescending tone, she would say, "That won't look good on you. You know it won't wash well and won't hold up. You can't have boots. Why in heaven's name would you pick that?" Not sure what heaven had to do with it. All of these made me feel vulnerable, stupid, and powerless. The seeds of shame are planted and fertilized.

Shame-dysfunctional family relationships.

Children that experience their parents fighting can result in feelings of shame. As a hypnotherapist, I've learned that parent's interactions when the baby is in the womb, can also impact their emotions even to adulthood.

This was the most difficult experience to share, which tells me it triggers my vulnerability. If you have been in this situation, I send you love. As you read, I hold space for your healing.

When they were fighting, I begged for them to stop. I worried and anticipated the fights coming and tried to prevent them to no avail.

This instilled feelings in me of being unimportant, blame, no opinion, and invisible. There was worry that I may have caused the fights. These all tie to shame and feeling worthless.

Shame-being the fun joyful self that I came into this world to be.
While in a store with mother, her friend, and my little friend, my friend and I went looking for toys. We found these different colored fuzzy hats. We put them on. Then we were dancing to our own music in our fun hats. Turns out our hats were commode seat covers.

Our mothers came to find us. My mother was certainly not amused. She yelled at me to stop and to act like an adult. Shame for expressing myself and having fun.

Wikipedia describes shame as: an unpleasant self-conscious emotion typically associated with a negative evaluation of the self, withdrawal motivations, and feelings of exposure, mistrust, powerlessness, and worthlessness.

Shame is a feeling brought on by conditioning. It resides in the conditioned self rather than the authentic self. When connected with the authentic self, there is no room for shame.

Initial feelings of shame are bestowed upon us from other people in situations where they project energy that creates an awareness of feeling like you have done something wrong or foolish. It is projected in a look, discipline, actions, or words. This exposure may come from parents, teachers, friends, society, or social media. The source may be from physical, sexual, verbal, and/or emotional abuse. The abuser may transfer their feelings of shame onto the victim.

The victim may feel that they somehow caused the abuse. The cycle spirals downward to a feeling that if one can trigger those actions in others, there must be something wrong with them. As they become an adult, they may avoid expressing feelings and especially anger. In many cases, anger is a healthy emotion. Anger suppression may lead to physical and emotional disease.

Feelings of worthlessness and having no value are a common effect of shame. It is often very subtle and hard to relate to but can be debilitating.

Shame may be an ancestral pattern, or feelings carried over from a past life. The shame may have occurred in another life related to beliefs or spiritual practices. As you become aware of this villain shame, you can heal. When you heal, you heal past, present, and future generations.

Shame may have external and internal triggers. After experiencing shame inflicted by others, it is possible to inflict shame on yourself. After all, it is then a familiar emotion. It may be destructive, but it is familiar.

Do any of the sentences below resonate with you or feel familiar?

- Shame on you.
- You should be ashamed.
- What would people think?
- You should know better.

How to shed the shame.

1. Connect with the feelings and explore them. Stuffing and fleeing from emotions are a negative influence of shame.
2. Journal

   1. Write how shame may have impacted your life. Let the words and feelings flow. Shame can present in holding back your voice, self-doubt, feeling unworthy, being distrustful, or other feelings.
   2. Write about specific situations. Where did it occur? How old were you? How did those experiences make you feel? Do you still hold the shame in your body?

3. Has the shame resulted in coping mechanisms? Coping can take on many faces. It may be withdrawal, perfectionism, distrust, or addictions.

4. Connect with your authentic higher self that knows the truth and is lovingly waiting to assist. Identify what was the truth of the experience.

5. Imagine giving the unwanted shame back to the perpetrators. It is their responsibility, not yours. You may also opt to release the shame to the Universe.

3. Hypnotherapy and coaching are powerful tools to explore and shed the shame. Contact me at Deena@acceptyourpower.com or call/text 623-810-2983.

Deena Chester

Deena Chester is an expert healer and owner of Accept Your Power. She is a bestselling author, certified hypnotherapist, past life regression specialist, ancestral eye reader, certified transformational life coach, Reiki Master, EFT practitioner, providing intuitive, transformational guidance for spiritual connection, past lives, and unique life purpose.

Deena's powerful blend of modalities and skills will help you live the life you were born to live. She offers individual sessions, workshops, online and by phone.

Email: Deena@acceptyourpower.com
Website: https://acceptyourpower.com
Facebook: https://www.facebook.com/acceptyourpower
Instagram: https://www.instagram.com/deena.chester

Scan Me

Family Jewels

by Denise Meyer

*"When meeting new people, always wear
the family jewels."*

~ Denise Meyer

Chapter 12

Family Jewels

by Denise Meyer

Today is the audition of my dreams! Twenty-plus years of experience in real estate and business coaching has earned me an audition for a coveted speaking position. This audience is the elite of the elite in my field.

I wear a red power dress and my family's jewels. My "Kundun mandala" necklace is a string of tokens worn by powerful women before me: my grandmother's diamond, my uncle's sapphire, my aunt's ruby, my great-grandmother's opal, and my mother's marriage bracelets are piled high. They don't necessarily match, but to me they are perfect.

I nod to the host.

I am excited, and I struggle to hold in my breakfast. I am numb to the introductions as I slide my hand to my Kundun mandala. I wear it with love around my neck as a talisman of good luck for the audition. It settles and grounds me. I sense a gentle whisper in my ear: "You were made for this. You are smart and talented and have much to offer. Just be you, and the right words will come effortlessly to bring value to your audience." I begin.

The women in my family, can be independent, they are also kind and truthful. Our family offers the power of tough love, and it works for us. We meet infrequently, yet we are tighter than the finest filigree in my grandmother's turquoise and pearl ring. When someone's world is falling apart, we circle and hold them until they can hold themselves again. My most important lessons have come from the strength of these women who raised me.

My mother, Tina, taught me unconditional love. My mother had not received the care and love that every small child deserves. I struggle to understand how one who never experienced pure love can so easily give me this precious jewel. She treated me with care and concern for my well-being, as if I were a precious stone that must be protected. But she did not lock me in a safe; she took me everywhere, and we did everything together. Just as I wear my family's jewelry always, I urge you to keep precious people and things close. Don't lock them away; keep the energy alive.

My mother taught me to say what needs to be said and to do it lovingly. When I was being counseled for a work challenge, I was expected to talk about my mother. At one point, the counselor said, "You have reason to be mad at your mother." I wasn't mad then, but after more counseling, my anger surfaced. I told my mother I was mad at her for some happenings during my childhood. "Oh Dee," she said, "I'm so sorry. Everyone knows it's the mothers fault."

Love is a defining word for me. When you are loved as a child, every challenge is surmountable. I give love and receive love, and it is like my family's jewels—not only for special occasions, but to be worn and cherished daily.

My sweet Tia Jill has taught me to be strong. When I was seventeen, she said "Dee Dee, you do not have to follow the path of anyone else. You get to choose who you will be." I pushed that advice away at the time, but now it is my foundation. It supports me to choose who I am and not to conform to anyone else's ideas, including hers. When sweet Tia Jill turned fifty, she said, "Dee Dee, let's go to the mall." Jill is not a mall shopper; what could we be shopping for? *I'm shopping for who I will become in the second part of my life.*

Jill and I share a love of jewelry. She re-designs, re-purposes, and creates unique jewelry, and I happily receive the jewels she adorns me with. I wear jewelry to represent who I choose to be and to honor from whom I come. The jewels instantly connect me to my ancestors' strength, love, and secret meanings conveyed in the sounds of the simple clinks of the rings or in the vision in the final mirror check.

My Grandma G taught me the importance of family. Her son, my father, had not much to do with me, yet Grandma and Grandpa G were powerful role models. I spent summers with them, and they cherished me and all the other grandchildren. They gave me a vision of my life: family around me in every circumstance.

Grandma G had four boys and always wanted a girl. As the first-born grandchild – and a girl, to boot, I had cherished rights. My butt never hit the ground as a baby. During the school year, life with my mom was quiet and one-on-one. I was treated as a little adult and had adult conversations. In the summer, I was pampered and treated as if I were a gift. We would visit the uncles, picking up my great-grandmother every Friday for dinner and returning her afterward to her little mobile-home park. We always went inside with her, and my grandma would poke the broom into every closet and under the bed for peace of mind.

I remember my grandma doing her makeup in the small bathroom of their ranch home in Northern California. She was done up in her pantyhose, sitting on the toilet lid talking to me. I felt like her best girl-friend. The year I turned fourteen, during one of our girl-talk times she said, "I have something for you." She pulled a long jewelry box from her drawer of special mementos. Inside was a special brown cloth, and delicately wrapped inside was a gold chain with five little gold spheres. "Your grandpa gave this to me," she said. "It's my favorite. I want you to have it." It is the most beautiful thing I've ever received, and I still wear it when I'm feeling delicate. It wraps me in the love of family, and I feel cherished.

There are seven auditions, and some go better than others. For each audition day, I wear the Kundun mandala lent to me by my sweet Tia Jill. "Dee Dee, wear this as a talisman to protect you with the strength of your family." She relays the history of the women who have worn the stones ("This black diamond was from your…"), each woman striving for a better life and a stronger family and loving those around her.

I'm biting my nails at a critical point in the audition process. This is the most challenging success I've ever pursued. Success, because I have earned the right and been chosen for the position that I and all the women I call family have worked for: *to have a voice.*

One day the Kundun mandala will be mine. I hope it will not be soon, as that would mean the passing of one of our own. I will wear it and share it with the women who come after me as a token to be strong, to choose your own path, and to always wear the jewelry!

Denise Meyer

Denise Meyer's favorite word is "Love," along with growth, joy, and prosperity. She often declares a word for the year. This mindset and passion have created many opportunities, from owning different businesses to coaching business- people to speaking across the United States. She initially fell into real estate sales after moving to a small town with limited jobs. She often wonders if her early teachers who wrote on her report card, "Denise is a joy to have in class if only she talked a little less," had taught her sales where she would be now! Her mentors taught her the importance of being a lifelong learner, and this set her down a path of success she feels fortunate to have experienced.

"I never finished college, though I went for a long time, and for too many years, I felt "less than". Then one day, I woke up and was over it. I realized I have taken more training and been coached for more hours with tremendous real-life experiences that I know enough and can always find the answer for the lessons to be learned." This awakening was super important for her next phase. She has coached over 21,000 coaching calls to business people, and taught over 1000 trainings, seminars, and classes. Her down-to-earth approach of speaking more of her failures than success will have you declaring… if she can do it, so can I.

https://www.youtube.com/watch?v=D7QnoHJJzuU&authuser=0
https://www.facebook.com/Denise-Meyer-Coach-100112048288661

Scan Me!

The Joys of Being a Chameleon

By Elizabeth Havlicek

*"Wisdom is not knowing how to make the right decision.
It is knowing how to 'make right' the decision made."*

~ Anonymous

Chapter 13

The Joys of Being a Chameleon

By Elizabeth Havlicek

"Oh, so you're a chameleon."

Initially, I was offended when the woman said that to me. I was in my twenties, quick to hear condescension in the words of an older stranger. What right did she have to tell me who I was? She didn't know me. All she had to go off of was my response to what I'm sure she thought was a simple question: Where are you from?

I tend to answer that question with a question of my own: "Originally, or most recently?" (Those answers, respectively: San Antonio, TX, and Upperville, VA.) Between San Antonio and Upperville, there have been 21 different addresses and countless experiences to pair with them between then and today.

To begin to tell anyone about who I am is a complex thing.

I could tell you about the woman who has no "real" home to go back to, the same woman who has people across seven different states and five different countries to welcome her "home" with open arms.

I could tell you about the woman who reached Global Services status on United Airlines, traveling over 250,000 miles a year, the same woman whose favorite place on earth was at home with her dog, regardless of where that home happened to be at the time.

I could tell you about the woman who has creativity in her blood, who graduated high school at 16, moved out at 17, and started off in design school in San Francisco, the same woman who grew up to be a turnaround and growth artist of manufacturing companies, who can think like an engineer and yet move people within those companies to find the best version of themselves and come together as a team to accomplish miraculous things.

I could tell you about the woman who could make tough decisions in difficult times, who personally laid off hundreds of people during the economic downturn of 2008, believing it wasn't a task that should be delegated, the same woman who had to drive to a mall parking lot and cry afterward, knowing the vulnerable position she had put those people in during a national financial crisis.

I could tell you about the woman who is twice divorced and sometimes feels incapable of sustaining long-term relationships. The same woman has an inexhaustible supply of love and lifelong friends around the world.

I could tell you about the woman who loves to throw parties for 100 or more people when often the only thing the guests have in common is their hostess, the same woman who freezes when invited to events where she does not know anyone.

I could tell you about the woman who stumbles over her words trying to make small talk, the same woman who can stand up in front of hundreds of people with a microphone and PowerPoint slides at industry conferences.

I could tell you about the woman who was asked to do a TEDx Talk called "The Power of Joy" as her whole life was seemingly falling apart around her after being betrayed in unimaginable ways by someone she loved, the same woman who used that TEDx Talk to help herself heal.

All of these women are in me, but none of them alone define me.

I was offended so many years ago by that chameleon comment because I took it to mean that I somehow was not authentic. I have come to wear it as a badge of honor instead.

A chameleon is not inauthentic — it is adaptive. It survives because it can easily change in new environments. I have allowed myself to take giant leaps and experience all of my complexities in different situations, accessing parts of myself I would never have gotten to know otherwise, all because I knew I had that ability to adapt. We all do.

That's not to say it's always easy. Every move, every new environment, has tested me. I know some people think I'm eccentric for living the way I do, so I tend to project certainty on the surface, even if underneath I feel terrified. When I know I'm following my instincts, though, the feeling of my heart pounding is my cue that I'm making the right choice. I see it as a zip-line adventure. I feel the fear and leap anyway.

What do people really need to know about being a chameleon?

The risks are worth the reward. There are so many joyful experiences I would have missed out on if I had skipped even one of my many moves. Being a chameleon and learning to adapt forces you to develop skills that many of us rarely get to exercise in a more stable life. You will not always succeed, but the lessons you learn are tremendous gifts for your soul's growth.

Of course, you do not have to be quite as eccentric as I have been. You have the power of the chameleon within you whether you've lived at 21 different addresses or the same place your entire life (even I hope for a final move and a forever home sometimes!) But try this: the next time you feel your heartbeat faster at the thought of making a significant change? Listen to it. Feel it. That's your adrenaline building up. Sure, you could use it to run away. Or you could use it to leap.

Elizabeth Havlicek

Life as a chameleon has been rich in experiences and long on learning. Elizabeth started in manufacturing, working her way up through various positions, much of the time in the Aerospace industry, but also in electronics and motorcycle garments and accessories.

She is currently the Managing Partner of a supplement company (www.phyto-quantusa.com).

She is also the Founder and Chief Cravings Creator of a confectionary company called Oooh So Good, LLC

(www.ooohsogood.com).

She has served on the boards of the Small Business Alliance, AZ, Operation Welcome Home, and the Arizona Wall Project (to build a scaled Vietnam War Memorial replica). In addition, she served on the board of Tedx Fountain Hills after having delivered two Tedx talks. (You can watch her talk titled the "Power of Joy" here:

The Power of Joy | Elizabeth Havlicek | TEDxFountainHills - YouTube)

She is currently residing in Tampa, FL, where she launched Oooh So Good, LLC. A portion of the profits from all sales of Oooh So Good products are donated to children's charities.

Daring to Ask

By Emma Porter

*"Mastering others is strength; mastering yourself
is true power."*

~ Lao Tzu

Chapter 14

Daring to Ask

By Emma Porter

There was something about becoming a divorced single parent who naturalized as an American citizen that meant I adopted beliefs that I "should not" ask others for help because that's not what I "should do."

May 2020 arrived and challenged those beliefs. It was time to practice a new skill. One of the most challenging times as an only adult in the home is when the body functions at a different rate than what you prefer. My level of physical pain felt out of this world. I was bedridden for several days, more than once.

I was determined to meet my first goal – walking myself to the bathroom within thirty minutes, something that usually only took a few seconds.

I ordered a pair of crutches. I cared not that I expressed my pain so vocally, bringing myself to a whimper when my school-aged sons inquired whether I was okay. This pain was my idea of hell on earth.

Fear can be paralyzing if left unmanaged. Time off work meant a loss of income, and I felt my independence and quality of parenting was under threat.

My thoughts slammed around my mind. What if my critics were right and my life was a train wreck about to happen?

I put pride to the side and asked on social media if anyone was available and willing to collect a prescription and some needed groceries. Without hesitation, responses appeared making it known who and how they could help. With the offers began a flow of conversation and self-reflection.

Asking for help was difficult, not just for me but for lots of other people, too! One friend asked, "Does it need to be an emergency for you to ask for help from another?" This friend wanted me to understand that very little was to be gained by denying myself a flow of receiving.

Soon, I received the opportunity to put the courage of asking for help in full swing. The pandemic isolated one of my dearest friends, my love. Initially, I thought my help would suffice, but it was as if the Universe was whispering to me, "Here's your chance!"

I felt fear again, yet I paused, reminded myself to stay present, researched, then reached out. The response was incredibly positive and one of transformation, with additional help from numerous sources, even from overseas!

I write this chapter because I would like you, the reader, to examine any self-limiting beliefs and judgments you may hold in asking for help. Perhaps have a conversation with those closest in your family and circle of friends. Challenge assumptions you may discover and upgrade any false or limiting beliefs. Please do not wait for a minor moment to turn into an emergency.

Since our arrival into this world as a newborn, we have accomplished so much with the help of countless others. Let us not take on the social conditioning that tells us there is some cut-off or boundary point in asking for or accepting help. If at first, you don't hear back, ask again using multiple resources. Be persistent! There are different avenues. For example, I learned of a non-profit organization comprised of volunteers who prepare their home-cooked lasagna and then deliver it to families – where a free, home-cooked meal can be the difference in having a good day or a challenging one. This organization reminded me of how the act of helping another, fills us up – to help without the expectation of anything in return.

What if you have depression or anxiety and you need help, but are afraid to ask for it?

I'm no stranger to the feelings of shame, perceived weakness, and the nagging storyline that I would be bothering someone else with my problems. This attitude, coupled with the exhaustion experienced from completing the simplest of tasks when not being physically well, only serves to keep our good from coming to us.

One thing I know for certain about depression or anxiety is that they lie. They suggest you're a failure and you're worthless. Those feelings will throw labels around the mind such as "lazy," "weak," "broken," "helpless," – the list goes on.

THAT IS ABSOLUTELY NOT TRUE!!!

Although these conditions can be serious, there are effective medical and alternative treatments that can assist with managing depression or anxiety.

Opening up about how you feel to those closest to you or to a professional can be an effective way to receiving the help and support you need. To start on a path of recovery requires courage. Dare to reach out! We ALL are deserving of support.

"Ask for help, not because you are weak, but because you want to remain strong" – Leslie Brown.

Emma Porter

Born in the United Kingdom, Emma Porter has also lived and worked in Sweden, Singapore and now in the United States. With her love of travel and people, Emma has been provided with extensive international experiences and perspectives that she applies to enhance a peaceful lifestyle. Emma currently works in correctional health, together with school-aged children.

Her passion is finding practical ways to encourage people to understand that their emotional well-being matters. She does this outside her day jobs through facilitating Dunisha "Zen" peace circles and using a modality called Chakradance™.

Emma is also a Never Binge Again ™Certified Professional Coach. She resides in Arizona, raising her children alongside their mischievous and loveable cockapoo and chihuahua. Emma can be contacted though her personal Facebook or at sverige_136@msn.com.

Scan Me!

Work in Progress

by Florine Duffield

"Be yourself; everyone else is taken."

~ Oscar Wilde

Chapter 15

Work in Progress

by Florine Duffield

I decided in the 2nd grade to work in the arts, and I stuck with it. After working in show business for many years, I decided I much preferred working on the other side of the camera. I went back to school and got a degree in photography. Many years later, I started painting with my father. My creative and professional life took on an additional offering into oil painting.

I call myself a portrait artist.

I divide my professional life between photography and painting. I take many classes and workshops. My brain is hungry to learn as much as I can to hone my skills. When I listen to what makes my heart sing – my work – I know that I am headed in the right direction. It has not always been easy. Being self-employed is not for the faint of heart! When you dream about your work and jump out of bed most mornings, that is a good indication that you are doing your life's work.

I also made a conscious decision to remain single and not to have children. I have always been self-sufficient and do not rely on others. Do not give away your power. Your time is more precious than money.

I am the perfect fit for a studio artist because I love working alone. Happiness is an inside job, I say.

I was recently with an art student providing encouragement and support on her work. Right in the middle of it all, she blurted out, "I love you!" I was really taken aback! It was a jolt of reality – a happy one, mind you. I feel it is my life's work to make people feel good about themselves. That has always been easy for me. I do that through my art and photography.

They say the most important legacy one can leave behind is how you make others feel. I aim to spread wisdom, knowledge, encouragement, and positive feelings to all I encounter. I was told by a well-known psychic that I heal people through my work. I will take that! I know where I am going and where I want to be; exactly where I am and who I am. However, just like some of my oil paintings, I am a work in progress.

It is important for me to know the purpose of your portrait. What are you trying to say about yourself? This will help enormously in getting your message out into the world. I strive to make people feel comfortable during our sessions.

When painting portraits, I work from photographs. I can create paintings of loved ones who have passed.

I continue to get work through word of mouth. They say I am a memory maker. We certainly have loads of fun during sessions!

I feel fortunate that clients respond favorably to my work. If I can help people feel better about themselves, then I feel I am successful. Comments from clients:

"Florine is very efficient, providing all the necessary details and answering all my questions promptly. She was very easy to work with. The photos were exactly what I was hoping for and she provided them within hours. I am extremely satisfied and highly recommend Florine."

"Florine is wonderful to work with. She is an amazing artist and photographer. I really appreciate her service and will work with her again."

"Florine is a very experienced professional who is so much fun to work with! Florine is genuinely interested in helping her clients achieve their best look, and she listened to my suggestions."

"Florine was wonderful, a consummate professional. Her photos were superb. I have been looking for someone to do a painting of my 99-year-old mother. After viewing her oil portraits, I decided to commission her for that project."

"Florine was very sweet and a blast to work with! My photos turned out great!"

"Florine was a pleasure to work with. She provided many excellent photos the same day of the shoot and offered to retouch them if necessary."

"Florine minimized my imperfections and highlighted my assets – not a simple feat – for which I am truly grateful. Her retouching skills are masterful!"

"Florine was gracious and gave me exactly what I needed. She was kind and listened to my project needs."

"We loved our experience with Florine. She made us feel relaxed. Her artistic talent is apparent in everything she does from photos to the prints to the portraits she paints. Florine puts her heart and soul into everything she does."

"The headshots Florine made of me were stunning. Florine really captured my personality and not just my picture. She really captured the essence of me, and they completely capture the message I am trying to get across."

"I could not have chosen a better professional than Florine to capture the essence of my beloved furball, Augie. I could tell she was thoroughly enjoying herself. It shows up in the results, which I shall always love and cherish."

"Florine gave me several hours of her time, using different outfits and many different lighting set-ups. I have a wide variety of beautiful headshots to choose from."

"Florine made a wonderful portrait of my dog, Benson. I was very impressed when she said she wanted to meet him in person to make additional photos so she could do justice to his true colors. The result was more valuable than words can express. He looks as though he could walk right out of the canvas. I will enjoy his portrait for many years to come."

The following list contains important bits of wisdom.

Approve of yourself. Allow yourself to be who you want to be. Do not look to others for approval – only from yourself.

Lighten up and have some fun!
Let go of anger. You are only hurting yourself.
Focus – this is an important one for me.
Make other people feel good.
Find comfort through the support of other women – be a good role model.
Keep your word – your promises are sacred.
Do not be fearful of the future.
Persevere – always step up to challenges.
Thoughts become things (choose the right ones) and things remain forever possible.
Judge no one – just improve yourself.
Be yourself, everyone else is taken.
Dream Big!

I think artists rule the world!

Florine Duffield

Florine Duffield began her education at Queens College and New York University, followed by Elkins Institute in Dallas and then Arvon Foundation in England. Her career began as a model, actress and singer in New York City. Ms. Duffield has been an accomplished photographer since the 1960s. She specializes in portraiture but includes animals and nature. Her father moved to Sun City, Arizona in the 1970s and, after visiting him many times over the years, she decided to move to Sun City permanently in 1999. She has owned and operated commercial photography and fine art studios in Dallas, New York City, Arizona, and England.

Years ago, Florine added oil painting to her creative expertise. She receives portrait commissions from humans, but also loves making portraits of her pet parrot, Max. She uses photo studies to create oil paintings onto linen or wood panels. Florine strives to capture the spirit of the subject in her portraits. The integrity of the subject's energy shines through. The background around the figure is an integral part of the completed artwork, where more information is revealed about the subject.

Phone: 623-565-0605
https://florineduffield.artstorefronts.com/

Scan Me!

Willing to Lead

By Jennifer L. Enos, D.D.S.

*Tell me, what is it you plan to do with this one
wild and precious life?*

~ Mary Oliver

Chapter 16

Willing to Lead

By Jennifer L. Enos, D.D.S.

I don't have a spectacular or amazing story. In all honesty, it is quite boring and typical. I am ok with that. It is a story of persistence and slow progress, the way most things in the world actually work.

My leadership story starts in Fourth Grade. Mr. McNamara was my teacher. Report cards came home, and, in the notes, it said, 'Jenny is more of a follower.' My mom explained what that meant and why it was important. I remember feeling hurt by the note. The final report card for the year came home with a note 'Jenny has developed into more of a leader than a follower.' The comments have stayed with me throughout my life. This was the foundation of my leadership journey, including in the dental profession. Reflecting now, I think about the value of 'following' in developing as a leader, in listening more than talking and asking lots of questions to lead effectively, and of patience and persistence, which I think Mr. McNamara might have missed in his initial assessment.

'Following' is one of the most effective ways to learn, and in my opinion, learning comes before leading. This is where having mentors comes in. A mentor is a teacher. Someone you can follow and learn from. For me, this started with my mother and father. Their relationship was one of equality and I watched my mother freely express her thoughts and opinions with my father's support. She demonstrated that this was ok. In my dental leadership life, it started with the dentist I worked for before dental school, Dr. Randy Regier, encouraging me to run to be the American Student Dental Association President. Explaining the benefits, I would receive and the opportunities I would have by putting myself out there. And, early on in my career, watching and getting the support of another young female dentist, Dr Allison House. She showed me I could do it and talked me through goals and challenges, providing the encouragement to keep progressing in a mostly male-dominated, significantly older boards.

Listening more than talking. Asking lots of questions. The listening is by far the hardest one for me and takes the most intention. But it has led me to many of my proudest accomplishments. One example is in bringing the Mission of Mercy, (one of the largest charitable events in Arizona) to Arizona. A dinner with colleagues from around the country allowed me to hear the story of the Colorado Mission of Mercy. It captured my attention with serving the dental needs of a large number of adults while bringing the dental community together. Although it was not initially adopted when I brought it to the board, a few years later others found the idea again and we were able to make it happen. My most recent project is a video series with stretches and core strengthening exercises for the dental community. This came from a dental assistant complaining of neck and back pain related to our work in dentistry and mentioning that she had to complete stretches before starting a shift when she worked for a burger joint. Just listening and asking questions allowed me to find another way to serve and lead our dental community.

Be persistent and patient. Most things don't happen as quickly and easily as we want them to. We have to stick with it until it happens. We must keep showing up. I started as the New Dentist Co-Chair for our local dental society. It took about 10 years to move up to President. I watched my older, male counterparts moved up in about 4 years. I had to continue to contribute meaningfully and keep showing up. It paid off. I became president (still one of the youngest and one of the few females) and then, when I demonstrated my capabilities, I moved much more quickly to President of the state Association (even faster than the older males).

At 43, I own a successful private dental practice, served as a District representative to the American Dental Association New Dentist Committee, served as President of our local dental society, served as President of our state dental association, served as a founder of the Central Arizona Dental Society Foundation Arizona Mission of Mercy, served as a delegate to the American Dental Association, and have recently founded Dental Longevity-the program for health and wellness of those in the dental field. I followed my mentors, listened, and asked lots of questions, and was persistent and patient. I encourage you to be willing to lead and just keep showing up.

Jennifer L. Enos, D.D.S.

Originally from Wyoming and Kansas, Dr. Enos earned her Bachelor of Science in Biology and Pre-Dentistry from Kansas State University. In 2004, she received her Doctorate of Dental Surgery from Creighton University in Omaha, NE.

She is the owner and a practicing dentist at Dental Arts of Chandler, AZ. She is also the founder of Dental Longevity, a program for the health and wellness of the dental team.

She is a member of numerous dental organizations including the American Dental Association, the Arizona Dental Association, the American Academy of Clear Aligners, the Pierre-Fauchard Academy, the American College of Dentists, and the International College of Dentists.

Dr. Enos served as the President of the Arizona Dental Association, the President of the Central Arizona Dental Society, a delegate to the American Dental Association, a representative to the American Dental Association New Dentist Committee, and a founding member of the Arizona Mission of Mercy.

Outside of dentistry, Dr. Enos enjoys traveling with her husband, Crossfit, and any fitness-related activities and helping rescue pups.

Where can you see more about and connect with me:

www.dental-longevity.com
www.dentalartsofchandler.com
LinkedIn: Jennifer Enos DDS
Instagram: Dental Arts of Chandler
Facebook: @dentallongevity

Life Lessons 101

By Joan Marlow

"Everyone is my teacher. Some I seek. Some I subconsciously attract. Often, I learn by observing others. Some may be completely unaware that I'm observing them, yet I bow with gratitude."

~ Eric Allen

Chapter 17

Life Lessons 101

By Joan Marlow

Life Lesson: noun…something from which useful knowledge or principles can be learned…

Wisdom: noun…abilities to discern inner qualities and relationships; good sense; generally accepted belief; accumulated philosophical or scientific learning; a wise attitude, belief or course of action

I didn't realize it at the time, but I had been 'studying' humans since I was a toddler and my inquisitive 2's never stopped. I still love asking 'why' and waiting for a response followed by clarifying questions to check my understanding. As I think about it, people don't often shy away from my questioning because it offers 'my teachers' a sense of importance that what they say matters (a basic human desire is to be listened to and 'heard' with heart and mind)…making eye contact helps as well.

'Life Lessons' are all around us, we simply need to be open and aware. My 60+ years of 'observing' and asking question's as I experienced my life and the lives of those around me offered informal 'data points,' that upon reflection, provided me a hypotheses of the existence of common threads that pass through all of us humans (aka 'the humanism of being human'). Our life experiences (stories) offer us the lessons we're meant to learn (wisdom). We all possess the same God-given human design and hardwiring to keep us alive and healthy. Our role is to nourish our physical, emotional and spiritual bodies to the best of our ability, which includes awareness of our thoughts, actions and relationships. Once we're 'aware' of a sensation, we can acknowledge it, choose an appropriate response and observe the outcome to determine if that outcome is best for us. If we discover the process to work, the 'wisdom' is to repeat it. We create a feedback loop for our greatest and highest good.

'Life Lessons 101,' serves as a foundational primer to support the health and wellbeing of your body, mind and spirit towards enhancing your joy and happiness and that of those around you. 'Life Lessons 101' is my 'wisdom' to pass along to support other's life journeys. How boring life might have been if we truly did learn everything we needed to know in Kindergarten?

We would have missed so many lessons along the way.

These five simple tools of Awareness (principles) and possible Actions will prepare you to consciously respond vs react to support your health and well-being. As you implement them, you'll create your own examples.

1. Be an Observer in Your Own Life...

Awareness: Have you ever gone blindly through your days on 'auto pilot?' When you eventually 'look up,' you realize you've missed...people, conversations, food, surroundings, let alone the subtle or not so subtle 'feelings/thoughts' that arise during a day. We seemingly keep moving forward until something forces us to stop...exhaustion, illness; a welcomed or unwelcomed 'bump in the road.' 'Observing' is a first step towards disengaging 'auto pilot,' living in the present moment, and taking time to honor what your body is telling you.

Action: Stop 3 times a day and 'observe' what's happening in your body and mind:

- Are your hands or jaw clenched? Is your back or neck stiff and painful? Is your stomach in knots?
- Note:
  - who you were just talking to; who might you be talking to next?
  - what was the most recent discussion topic?
  - what 'feelings' / sensations (anxious, tired, distracted, happy, excited, dis-ease) are present?
  - where are you feeling it?

After you've made these observations for a couple of days, see if there's a pattern. You're discovering some of your personal stressors… *THEN,*

2.   Decide What You Can Control and What You Can't, Know The Difference and Act Accordingly…

Review the list you've created from Lesson 1 and sort your findings into two columns…what you can control and what you can't control.

Awareness to Action:
If:
- one of the things you discover boils down to 'worry,' remember that 'action,' not 'worry' resolves issues…if you have no control to reach resolution, let it go; if you can impact a resolution, then figure out a way and do it.

- a person or discussion topic (or too much coffee), is causing you 'discomfort/dis-ease,' you might have to adjust the relationship with the person, remove the topic from future discussions or adjust your diet.

- you're frustrated while attempting to 'change' someone, cease and desist...the 'ONLY' person you can control is YOU! Including control of your responses/reactions with this person by following the bullet above.

3.   Where The Mind Goes, The Body Follows...So Keep it Positive...

Awareness: Thoughts are a form of energy and energy is what fuels all that we do and are. We're surrounded by energy...ours and others. Positive breeds positive; negative breeds negative... attitude, people, choices. The more positively you live, the more positivity you'll attract. Be alert to the fact that what you attract might not be in the format you expected...observe, acknowledge and say thank you.

Action:

- Surround yourself with positive people, activities and topics.
- Create healthy boundaries to keep you safe from 'energy vampires,' individuals who might not have your highest good at heart (Lesson 2).
- Implement a practice of gratitude: List 3 things you're grateful for each day. Better yet, keep a gratitude journal which is helpful on those 'not-so-good' days when reviewing your journal can remind you of things you're grateful for.
- Use affirmations: positive statements of fact that when repeated over time, your body, mind and spirit believes as true. I am

enough; I am smart; I am happy, healthy, wealthy and complete; things are always working out for me; it's all good, because it is.

- Learn to say 'NO' without guilt because you're worth it!! The more you say 'NO' to things that don't serve your greatest and highest good, the more you can say 'YES' to things that do.
- Stay 'in the present' moment…if your mind is hijacked, you can bring it back to this moment.

4.   Just B-R-E-A-T-H-E . . .

Awareness: The act of breathing is automatic…that's both good and bad. We know when one breath is complete, another one follows without any conscious thought. However, when we 'consciously' breathe, we expand the lower lungs, oxygenate the blood more effectively, and literally 'reset' our nervous system from fight/flight/freeze to rest and digest. Our body automatically relaxes, which allows our bodies to heal.

Action:

- Stop what you're doing and consciously take a slow, deep breath into your belly (count of 6); hold it (count of 4); exhale it completely (count of 6). Take 3 of these breaths 3 times per day and
- *Notice* the difference. You've neutralized and shut down the release of cortisol and adrenalin (stress hormones) and made way for dopamine, serotonin, oxytocin, and endorphins (good hormones) to pour through your body

5.   Open Your Mind to New Perspectives…

Awareness: Perspectives are the lenses we use to create our beliefs. They come from parents, teachers, schools, and more. The question to ask is: Is this belief serving me well?

Action:

- Challenge your Belief System!!
- Go out and learn something new!!
- Congratulate yourself for choosing this book as you welcome many points of Wisdom and perspectives into your life!!
- What will you choose to implement?

Namaste

Joan Marlow

Life has been my classroom; the people and experiences of my life have been my teachers.

I am…

- a 'lifelong learner and a forever teacher' with an insatiable curiosity for new perspectives to support my growth and awareness.
- fueled by an unquenchable thirst for life.
- forever positive and believe that anything is possible.
- a Jersey girl who doesn't take 'no' for an answer…I'll figure it out.
- Joan Marlow, open, honest, and fun (my personal power statement).
- living my passion & purpose as a life & wellness coach, educator and alternative health practitioner in my business, Peaceful Easy Healing assisting you with your health and wellbeing needs.

Eclectic people, interests and experiences are my favorite source of energy. "Just BREATHE…" is my mantra and way of life. "Things are always working out for me," is my affirmation revealing itself often.

My formal education is Education; informal education is 'never being afraid to ask 'why.' My path has been teacher; trainer, mentor, and manager in corporate America; then responding to the hypnotic draw of entrepreneurship 20+ years ago. My focus is to share Awareness and offer practical tips, tools, and techniques to reduce stress and live a balanced life; your role is to 'choose' to take Action to support creating your best life.

I love all things beach. I adore my cat, Kali, who is my able-bodied assistant supporting my self-care and my clients' healing.

www.peacefullyhealing.com
joan@peacefullyhealing.com
https://www.facebook.com/PeacefulEasyHealing/
https://www.linkedin.com/in/joandmarlow/
https://www.youtube.com/channel/
UCs51Lw9z61SHMo6AFWJ2Dyg

The Healing Gift of Opposites

By Judith Manganiello

*"When you own and embrace Your Wisdom Self,
Grace will flow naturally through you in a
Radiant Loving Way."*

~ Judith Manganiello

Chapter 18

The Healing Gift of Opposites

By Judith Manganiello

Opposites are the basis of humanity's operating system. They provide necessary contrast for us because everything in life offers a reason, a lesson, and most of all, a gift! I am grateful to be learning and growing in wisdom every day – thanks to the perspective I get from seeing positives, negatives, and what's in between. Then, when I get out of my own way – my next lesson arrives.

I notice the gift in everything and everybody. When I feel resistance, I know there is a situation of opposite forces. If one part of the situation bothers me, I know it is mine to heal. I say that to myself and to everyone who shares with me what is irritating them.

What I know for certain is that people do not have to survive tragedy, problems, or negativity to realize their full strength. I wish every child would learn this. If everyone were taught during youth to recognize, work with, and balance their emotions, there would be no more bullies, martyrs, or victims.

You and I have the ability to claim our powers of resilience right now. It is waiting right inside of you. Take your power back and shine!

Negativity and tests bother me for as long as I want to hold on to them in my soul consciousness. They might be from this life or from whatever lifetime I choose to examine. After all, I have free will and choice down here in the human experience. There are always plenty of ways to heal any situation – you just have to take the time and have the patience to find them.

For example, my husband Lou and I are complete opposites. I am always a peacemaker, and he is the peace officer (he worked for the police department). My cup runs over with happiness and love. His cup is half-empty, or sometimes, totally drained. I see everything in its order. He sees everything that is out of order because that was his job. Spirit advises that opposites attract because they teach people what they need to learn about healing themselves. Lou has been my opposite gift for 48 years and counting. Thanks to him, I have learned almost all the lessons I came to Earth to learn. Maybe he has, too!

The gift of seeing opposites goes beyond what you experience with a partner. It could also be reflected through your family or friends – and even sometimes with a stranger.

As a child, when I hugged someone, there were always 'hug collisions.' I'd bump into people's noses, sometimes knock off their glasses. I thought that was strange... I seemed to be the only one having these hug collisions. It wasn't until after I was gifted the store that I understood: I received awareness that my hugs were heart-to-heart.

And then, while writing about opposites, that I was given the message behind the heart-to-heart hugs. Everyone I hugged was avoiding the heart and resisting the balance that occurs when two opposite people engage in a hug. I saw how everyone usually hugged with their right (or male) side to the other's right (male) side. The heart is on the left side of the body, so they avoided a heart connection and did not unite all sides together to create a full-on, balanced hug, with Spirit in the center of both of their hearts. Spirit is in the center of everyone.

Now that you have this wisdom, I encourage you to embrace the balance of hugging with your male, female, and Divine Spirit-Self. That's the *real* reason people choose to hug one another!

Spirit reminds me: "We create everything that is going on in our lives, the good, the bad, or the ugly." I certainly did not believe that was true when I was younger. As I started learning how and what I was creating and ways to take my power back to clear and release it all, my life became happier. This was when I became much more grateful about being here in physical form. It gets better and better every day I am alive.

In living over 70 years on this beautiful planet Earth, I've learned I have both female and male energies in me as part of my Divine Spirit-Self. I know I have a team of guides within me who help me all along my way. They're ready, willing, and able to assist me on this wonderful yet sometimes challenging journey.

I came into this world apparently only using my female side. I trusted everyone and was so gullible. I didn't understand why anyone could choose to lie. That was exactly the way I thought. I always wanted – and still want – to hear the truth, even if it hurt, even if it meant losing a friend.

My female side does not know how to say no. She stills wants to help and give everything to everyone. Now that I have finally given him a voice, my male side can say no with the loving energy he receives from my female side of awareness. After all, they both get their wisdom from my Divine Inner Spiritual Self.

Here is a prayer that helps me to know what to trust: "God or Spirit, I choose that your voice will be my first thought, and I will trust you." When you say this prayer and ask a question, Spirit always provides the answer. Do not overthink it; always trust the first answer that comes to you as it is Spirit giving you what you asked for. You only have to say this once; afterward, you just have to trust the first message.

The Spirit of your female side will be open to receive and listen to the Divine Inner Guidance from within. She is there to learn and know what side is talking to her. But there is also your human ego female side. When faced with a problem, your female ego will feel hurt, disappointed, and sad about the outcome.

Your male Spirit side must believe he has a voice with the strength and energy to get it done, all with grace and ease. This voice will not come from anger or frustration as long as the guidance comes from the Divine Inner Spirit-Self. When the voice is coming from your male ego human self, you will feel anger, be upset, and general feelings of unhappiness. It is extremely important to make sure all your Inner Wisdom sides are being heard and are working together as a team.

Now that I am listening and working with all the wisdom within me – male and female, ego and Spirit – I finally realize there is nothing I cannot do! Just as sweet, salty, spicy, and bitter flavors can work together with the right energy recipe, opposites can unite as a team.

You can create everything and make all your dreams come true with grace and ease in zero Earth time. Being in harmony with the universe is when you love and appreciate your entire existence with your Divine inner oneness.

Judith Manganiello

At age 38, Judith met her "Inner Light" and went on to open A Peace of the Universe, a Spiritual book and gift store in Scottsdale, in 1992.

A numerologist, an open channel with Spirit and the Angelic realm since childhood, Judith teaches self-love and how to take your power back. Known for giving powerful, healing hugs and transformational guidance, Judith wrote and published,

A Giver's Way Home: Journey for Self-Love after retiring in September 2016.

Email Judith to receive a personalized, autographed copy.

To learn more, you can reach Judith at:
Judith999apotu@gmail.com
http://judithandspirit.com/index.html

The Search for God

By Judith McClure

"No matter what they tell you,
No matter what they do
No matter what they teach you
What you believe is true.

~ From the song "No Matter What" by Boyzone

Chapter 19

The Search for God

By Judith McClure

I think we sometimes first have to learn who God isn't before we actually learn who God is!

My search for God began as a young child when I left a piece of candy under my pillow and told God that if He really exists, He would take that candy as proof. How elated I was to wake up and find the candy gone – then I found it on the floor!

This only intensified my search further. The fourth time I was to be baptized, the minister instructed me to bring my mother. It was hard getting her out of bed on a Sunday morning. "But Judy, you've already been baptized three times," she said. "I know mom," I shouted excitedly, "but this is a new church!"

I didn't get baptized for fear of not being saved. I got baptized so many times because if I heard the song, *"Softly and Tenderly Jesus is Calling,"* I ran down the aisle crying. The minister's pleading for someone to come and be baptized only made me run faster! I thought Jesus really was calling me.

Many of my questions about God could not be answered in mainstream religion. One Sunday morning, after a very uncomfortable and judgmental sermon telling us we were all sinners, I walked out the door and said, "God, if you would send me to Hell for searching for You, I am willing to spend eternity in Hell. I can't find You here." (I have to add here that, for a period of time, I regretted that statement and began to worry that indeed "He" might just send me there!)

I wandered Godless for a while and began reading books on reincarnation, spirituality and Dr. Raymond Moody's book, *"Life After Life."* Things were beginning to make sense for me!

Then one day, a cult came through our little town in Florida. On the hotel marquee, it said, "Do you believe in reincarnation, UFOs, Angels?" and a few other things. Boy, did I! I had to attend that lecture.

I was invited to their spirit meeting, where God himself, Yahweh, spoke to me personally through a channel. He said, "My dear, you have searched and searched for a long time, and now you have finally found." Wow! I was one hundred percent sure I had found God! Since I was recently divorced, I was free to leave with the Yahweh group when they moved first to Mississippi, and then to Phoenix.

It was while in Mississippi that I began noticing the Yahweh group was very much out of integrity. The things Yahweh was channeling didn't sound very loving. The entire eleven months my teenage daughters and I were with this group, I had recurring dreams of swimming in muddy water.

We were in Phoenix only for a short time when the Yahweh group decided to move again. I had given away everything I owned except my car, had almost lost custody of my daughters, had no job and now I no longer believed in Yahweh. We parted ways and I was Godless again!

I think when you are meant to be somewhere, you will be. Phoenix literally opened its' arms to me. An apartment complex let me in with only one month's rent, no deposit and no job. The previous tenants left behind rental furniture that wasn't picked up for over a month. The day it was picked up, the manager appeared with bits and pieces of furniture other tenants had left behind.

My daughters babysat children in our complex and gave me their babysitting money for gas to search for work. In a mild recession, I found a job.

I had arrived! Phoenix was a smorgasbord of spirituality. I bought my first crystal, went to psychic fairs and took classes from some of Phoenix's best spiritual teachers. Audrey Hunt taught me how to connect with God through listening and writing. Rev. Dr. Gary McClure, the man I would later marry, taught me healing. Ann Albers taught me how to manifest my heart's desires and Rev. Dehbra Taylor was my mentor. How awesome could it get! All of my teachers taught and showed me that God is Love.

I have been widowed now for twenty-four years and live in a quiet little town on the banks of the Suwannee River. I have made peace with religion. I know each person has to find God in their own way and follow their own path. I have come to the understanding that God is within and in everything.

I like the way P'taah, channeled by Jani King, phrases it: "We are expressions of Divinity." And so, I am!

Rev. Judith McClure

Rev. Judith McClure is the director of The Center for Expanding Consciousness, a small spiritual center where eighteen ministers facilitate their own practices.

She is a contributor of several short stories published in Kay Allenbaugh's book series, *"Chocolate for a Woman's Heart."* Judith co-authored, *"Mommy, Someone's Touching Susan"* and is the author of, *"I Trusted Him,"* a series of books written about child molestation to help empower children.

Judith is the owner of a Bed & Breakfast in a 120-year-old Victorian House, which is walking distance to the Suwannee River. She is also a Trail Angel to hikers on the Florida Trail. In her free time, she paints flowers on hundred-year-old windows, mermaids on bottles, and makes wonderful treasures from junk people put out on the sides of the road! She is also seen, quite often, playing ball or Frisbee with her eight-year-old great-grandson, Malachi Jayce!

Website: https://whitespringsbnb.net
Email: whitespringsbnb@hotmail.com

In This Peace

by Junie Swadron

*"If you did not write every day, the poisons would
accumulate and you will begin to die, or act crazy, or both.
You must stay drunk on writing
so that reality cannot destroy you."*

~ Ray Bradbury – Zen and the Art of Writing

Chapter 20

In This Peace

by Junie Swadron

Recently, my beloved partner, David, was concerned about me. I was unable to sleep most nights and was operating on empty.

After Covid 19 started, having lost my 'in-person' book coaching business, I had to dance as fast as I could to find a way to get it online and then find people to register. Two things I find the most frustrating in my work – tech, and marketing!

With the help of dedicated people, I managed both. The week before my Author Mentorship Program was to begin, with 18 people registered, I chose to take a much-needed holiday. I chose to go to a 26-acre retreat centre cradled by two lakes with forest trails throughout the property. It would require taking a ferry from Victoria to Vancouver, then driving about two hours, and then hopping on another ferry at Horseshoe Bay to Bowen Island - a tiny, remote island off the Coast of Vancouver Island.

David drove me there but had to return home the next day. That night, nestled in our cabin in the woods, I woke at 4:50 a.m. in absolute turmoil wanting the world to go away! I needed more than four days – I needed to get off the never-ending treadmill for at least a month.

I knew it was impossible. I had to show up and facilitate my new online program. I couldn't sleep so I went over to my computer to check some details of the course and woke David in the process. Frustrated, I returned to bed. David sat up and stated,

"Junie, if you don't take advantage of this time here and breathe in the peace of this land, I will take your computer and your cell phone with me when I leave."

I told him, equally emphatically, that I would hide his car keys.

He stayed silent awhile, then offered me what he knew would be the sure "fix" that would transform my anxiety and funk. He reached over, handed me my journal and said, "Here. Now write."

I didn't want to. I wanted to whine. Belligerently, I got out of bed, went to the small desk, put on the desk lamp, and wrote from the prompt he offered me, *In this peace, I shall....*

And as always, I am so grateful I did. How else will I ever know the truth? I cannot. It is writing that brings me home to myself, without fail - each and every time.

In This Peace, I shall...

In this peace, I shall find God.

In this peace, I shall find me.

In this peace, I will unravel. I will twist and turn and be shoved and shaken, and in this peace, I shall not resist.

I will not hang onto rugged branches that jut out from the banks. I will not grasp onto their temporary refuge from the raging rapids. No, I shall let the river take me to and fro – winding down and around its billowing unpredictable forcefield.

I surrender here fully even though my heart is pumping faster than hurricane blood – coursing, exploding through this body's fragile temple – lungs infused with God's purest prana. I know even though this unstoppable force is leading me to destinations unseen, unknown and uncharted, never before have I felt this safe.

In these rapids, I shall find a peace that surpasses all understanding, and I shall rest here. Here I AM the eye of the storm – an impartial witness in waters gone mad, born of lost dreams and uncertainty. Yet I AM Still. I AM Peace.

Did I really think my puny hands, no matter how tightly I clenched them, would save me? Such naivete.

I am ready to see, feel and know myself as the God I AM. I AM ready to drop the scales from my eyes and open them as a newborn baby does, seeing the world and its majestic splendor for the very first time.

I AM that baby. Born anew. Curious, joyful, unstoried, free! Yes, the raging rapids of my life could have bounced and broken me against a million boulders, smashed me into shards of glass, rendering me defeated, hopeless, dead even.

Instead, the waters in all their compassionate glory opened their arms to this inner river's untamed fury – infusing the turmoil with gentle, rocking motion – a lullaby quieting the unrelenting noise –the torture chamber of the mind shapeshifting me from high alert into unsuspecting emptiness and grace. Pure exhaustion finally surrendered itself, its last grasp of holding on only to arrive naked upon pristine beaches – Mother Earth's welcoming breast seducing me into deep, peaceful slumber, washing clean all that went before.

And when I woke, it was as though a thousand nights had passed. Rested. Restored, Rendered Brand New bearing witness to Heaven on Earth.

Here I vowed to walk with the angels and saints who carried me here. I vowed to remain humble in this glorious land of Eden. Here I now taste the palate of milk and honey, ready to savour its gifts in sustainable ways.

And I shall walk among others who have survived bruises too horrific to name. They too had raging river rapids now transformed into calm blue seas, and it is here that we meet and recognize one another – Our Tribe – and it is our mission to walk together to shine our Gratitude, our Love and our Light. We walk fearlessly hand in hand into storms, calming the seas of disquiet for all those ready to walk among us and know the Promise and the Peace of God that beats our collective hearts as one.

In this Peace, we walk together co-creating with our Maker

In this Peace, we find Truth

In this Peace, we are One

In this Peace, we are Love

In this Peace, we are Home

Addendum:

I was a child without a voice. It was not safe to speak out at home, but I discovered my diary. It was my safe place. The only place. I had no idea that little red book with its lock and key that I found at the age of 11 would become my lifeline and has continued to be such my entire life.

Eventually, I realized that the writing strengthened me. Words, thoughts, ideas, beliefs flowed out of my pen that my subconscious had, up until then, kept in hiding. The more I wrote, the more I learned about myself. The writing soon enough gave me the courage to speak out. It took decades – but the woman I am today does not resemble the person I was for more than the first half of my life.

Today I am a psychotherapist, writing coach and teach others the magic of the pen. My motto, which comes from true lived experience, is this: *"Your soul meets you on the page, and something shifts. You strengthen. You begin to stand stronger. Then one day, you notice that your voice on the page becomes your voice in the world."*

If you don't believe me, you must pick up your pen and try it yourself.

And if you still aren't convinced, heed Ray Bradbury's words,

"If you do not write every day, the poisons would accumulate, and you would begin to die, or act crazy or both. You must stay drunk on writing so reality cannot destroy you."

Junie Swadron

Junie Swadron is an author, playwright, psychotherapist, international speaker, workshop facilitator, and professional writing coach who has spent the last thirty years guiding thousands of students in writing and sharing their life stories.

She sees the therapeutic process and the creative process as one. "It is about accessing a special place within us where serenity, love, courage, and truth reside. It is from this place that we begin to know our true spirit. It is from this place we begin to heal."

What makes Junie's approach to healing extraordinary is that she knows both sides of the couch. On her own healing journey, Junie found writing to be her greatest ally. She now shares her success with her clients and students, helping them connect to their creativity and healing through the written word and other modalities.

Junie resides in Victoria, British Columbia, Canada with her partner, David Halliwell, an artist and musician. They are currently co-creating a musical called *Today* and looking forward to cutting the ribbon for the Academy of Creative and Healing Arts.

Visit the website: https://junieswadron.com | https://junieswadron.com/mental-health
Contact Junie Swadron: junie@junieswadron.com

Scan Me!

The Wisdom of Discerning Between "Just Is" and "Justice"

By Karen Malta

*"Fight for the things that you care about,
but do it in a way that will lead others to join you."*

~ Honorable Ruth Bader Ginsburg,
Associate Justice of the Supreme Court of the
United States

Chapter 21

The Wisdom of Discerning Between "Just Is" and "Justice"

By Karen Malta

Congratulations! If you are reading this, you are a survivor of COVID-19, a "Just Is" epidemic. This virus has indiscriminately impacted us not only physically, but financially, emotionally and politically. I lost my beloved soulmate and husband, John, to COVID-19 on January 27, 2021. This writing is dedicated to him and our eternal love. My prayer is by sharing from the deepest part of my heart I will inspire you to rise up and thrive in spite of the "Just Is" challenges impacting you.

I am also a survivor of cancer, child abuse, sexual assault, domestic violence, bullying, and sexual and workplace harassment. I've come to learn the never-ending strength and courage it takes to be a surviving warrior of "Just Is." Pain is part of the plan. It's inevitable. But we have choices. We can wallow around as paralyzed victims, suffocating in darkness and toxicity, or we can reach out, rise up and thrive by being curious and making "Connections that Matter." By making caring connections with my Savior, Jesus Christ, angels, my health care providers and treasured friends, I have not only survived, but I have thrived and am stronger than I ever thought possible. You too can overcome pain and be surviving warriors.

Let me share my correlation and perspective of "Just Is" and "Justice." One definition of **Justice** is: n. **1) Justice is fairness in the way people are treated.** 2) moral rightness. 3) a scheme or system of law in which every person receives his/her/its due from the system, including all rights, both natural and legal.

For nearly four decades, I have diligently served to help ensure the integrity and independence of our third branch of government, the judiciary. Countless times I have been the voice for the public and court staff who have been innocent victims of poor case management practices, unethical conduct by superiors (yes, including judges), harassment, criminal activity, and sexual assault. I have a passion for serving in the judiciary, and I believe, while not perfect, our system is the best in the world. It provides us with the opportunity to have a voice and be change makers to improve society. I love how families who have been victimized by "Just Is" circumstances have utilized our "Justice" system to enact new legislation to not only honor their loved one but put into place laws to improve our system and reduce the likelihood of others falling victim to "Just Is" circumstances.

In July 2013, the Black Lives Matter Movement began after the acquittal of George Zimmerman in the shooting death of African-American teen Trayvon Martin 17 months earlier in February 2012. The movement exploded to new heights in 2020 after witnessing the death of George Floyd,

on May 25, 2020. Friends and family impacted by this horrible tragedy chose to be a voice and make a difference to not only honor George Floyd, but strive to help prevent others from unjustly dying at the hands of police. On March 3, 2021, H.R. 1280, the George Floyd Justice in Policing Act of 2021 was passed by the House of Representatives. It is a bill that addresses a wide range of policies and issues regarding policing practices and law enforcement accountability.

Another perspective of "Justice" is the way we process situations, circumstances, and people whom we believe have been unjust or unfair to us. It could be a spouse, friend, family member, co- worker, or neighbor that has treated you badly. I have experienced unfairness from all of these, but the worst was what I experienced from family members. What I have learned is forgiveness is critical to surviving "Just Is" circumstances and brings more peace and joy into my life. There are countless references to forgiveness in the Bible.

Matthew 6:14 states:

"For if ye forgive men their trespasses, your heavenly Father will also forgive you."

A psychology definition of Forgiveness is:

"Letting go of past grudges or lingering anger
against a person or persons.
The intentional and voluntary process by
which one who may initially feel victimized,
undergoes a change in feelings and attitude regarding a
given offense and overcomes
negative emotions such as resentment and vengeance
(however justified that may be.)

Through true forgiveness I believe we can release negative and toxic energy towards others and gain an acceptance that others may simply not be capable of realizing or not care about how their actions impact us. No matter how much we may want their love and acceptance, we cannot change them. It "Just Is" what it is. Rather than continue to try and have a relationship with people that reject and abuse you, it is best to accept them as they are and move on. Instead, surround yourself with kind, loving, positive people.

I love the quote by Wes Moore during an Oprah Super Soul Sunday episode:

"Don't let people that don't matter too much, matter too much."

Show your heart "Justice," by accepting what "Just Is" about others. Send toxic people on their way with love and forgiveness. Seek "Justice" for yourself by choosing to love yourself enough to embrace forgiveness not only for others, but for yourself too. Take action and be your best self by showing up in the world and aligning yourself with causes and people that matter most to you. These are "Connections that Matter."

One of the essential "Connections that Matter" is the connection you make within yourself. This requires connecting your head and your heart. This connection can be hard, but it's imperative to living a purpose-filled life.

There are countless strategies and techniques to help you connect your head and your heart, including prayer, meditation, counseling, and yoga. Be curious and explore what feels right for you. Be still and listen to your heart. Keep a journal by your bedside and write down whatever comes to your mind. Be sure to include things you are grateful for. From getting a parking spot to appreciating the beauty of a sunset; it all matters. Sometimes it can be difficult to quiet your mind and be still. I get it! Breathe, be still, listen and surrender. I find praying critical to my life and communicate with my Heavenly Father countless times throughout the day. It helps me feel grounded and in alignment with my purpose and calling as "The Caring Connector." Connect with me at www.TheCaringConnector. com for more information and ideas on ways you can discover your passion and purpose.

Simultaneous in striving to be grounded and listening to my heart, I align myself with people I deem to be successful. Who do you know that is successful? Oprah, Bill Gates, and Richard Branson come to my mind. Do you think they became successful alone? Not a chance! They all made "Connections that Matter," and so can you! I invite you to join my community of Caring Connectors on Facebook at https://www.facebook.com/Thecaringconnector.

Time is so precious, and living with joy, grace, and passion is priceless. We all are worthy and deserve joy and happiness. Together we can and will make a difference. We are survivors of "Just Is," and by making "Connections that Matter," we can (and should) seek "Justice."

Karen Malta

Karen has 40 years of experience and is known around the world as *"The Caring Connector,"* an advocate for justice, and a passionate spokesperson for victims and philanthropic causes. She is a sought-after expert in showing people how to live a purposeful life, and manifest joy and wealth by making *"Connections that Matter."*

Karen loves "serving without strings." Through her *"Angels Fly Forever"* project, she has designed and delivered over 3,000 angel dolls to those in need around the globe. She, along with her pet dogs and fur babies, Sprinkles and Buttons, passionately host youth serving the Lord by managing *"The Malta Ranch for Missionaries."*

Karen is a TV Spokesperson, International Speaker, Best-Selling Author, Business Consultant, and Global Entrepreneur. She has appeared on TV stations affiliated with ABC, CBS, and FOX news as an inspirational expert and advocate against abuse and domestic violence. She also appears on television and radio – raising thousands of dollars for community, national and international philanthropic organizations, including *Make-A-Wish, Phoenix Children's Hospital*, and many Veterans organizations.

Karen served as a Facilitator for *The World Academy for the Future of Women* and created *"The Global Circle of Champions"* – 10 international experts who presented with United Nations Leaders at the 9th Annual Women's Symposium at the Sias International Campus in Xinzheng, China.

This writing is a tribute to her beloved husband, John Malta, who lost his battle with COVID-19 on 1/27/2021. Karen is a survivor and believes through God's grace we can turn our messes into messages of hope and triumph over tragedy.

Email: TheCaringConnector@gmail.com
Web: www.TheCaringConnector.com
Facebook: https://www.facebook.com/Thecaringconnector

Scan Me!

The Lens You Use...
Determines the Maps You Choose

by Kimberly Allain

Success should not cost you what you value
and who you love!

~ Kimberly Allain

Chapter 22

The Lens You Use...
Determines the Maps You Choose

By Kimberly Allain

Finally grabbing my computer bag and keys, locking up the building and heading out to my car. It is late and dark. I am tired and I still have work to do when I get home. I turn the corner and standing in the dark next to my car is my husband. When I get to him, he asks me what time it is. I look at my watch and say 10:30. He looks at me for a moment, takes a deep breath and asks, "When do the boys and I get some of you?" I got angry and started telling him how busy I am, how important the work I'm doing is and that I still had more work to do when I got home. He simply looked at me and then turned, walked away and left me standing there. I got in my car feeling angry and unappreciated.

Driving home, I replayed what happened over and over in my head. I pulled into the driveway turned off the car and sat there staring at a dark house. I knew that when I walked in, our boys would be sleeping. I thought once again about the question my husband had

167

asked, "When do the boys and I get some of you?" I sat in that car and cried silently feeling like a failure. There was not enough of me to go around. Either work suffered or my family. He was right. My family got what was left of me, crumbs. It felt like a no-win situation.

I went inside and everyone was in bed. I threw my computer bag on the table and walked upstairs to our room. My husband was lying in bed watching TV. He looked at me and I said, "I don't know how to fix this. How did my life get this out of control? This is not how I want our life to be." He got up and put his arms around me and silently held me. Then I looked at this incredible man and committed to figuring this out. Success should not cost you what you value and who you love. It almost cost me both. Never again!

I was giving my best and striving to create change in my organization and community. I was really good at it and the results were creating positive change. I was focused on creating possibilities and serving others and I loved it. I asked myself, "How that can be wrong?" The truth is that it wasn't wrong at all. So, how did I get so off course?

This was a turning point question. How did I get so off course? What course was I on? What map was I using?

Have you ever found yourself in a situation and wondered how in the heck did you got there? Or been at a crossroads and felt like you wanted to make a change but wasn't sure what to do, or which way to go? Ugh! So frustrating!

As you can see, I have certainly been there, too!

What to do? Here are three things I learned that helped me make the shift in my life:

1. The first is about the lens that we see and interpret the world through. I think intellectually, we all know that each of us perceives the world or a situation from our own particular perspective or lens. But here's the thing: How conscious are you of the lens you're looking through? Are you consciously

choosing the particular lens that you want to apply in each situation or decision?

2. The second thing is that the lens you're looking through directly impacts the maps you choose to use in making decisions and taking action. This makes sense if you think about it. How you see something is a critical data point for making decisions and taking action. What maps are you using to navigate your life?

3. The third thing is that the lens you use also impacts how you show up in any given situation. How you are thinking, and feeling is communicated automatically.

Looking at my situation, the hardest part was getting honest about the lens I was using to create my world.

I discovered the lens I was using was that sacrifices were required, or failure was the result. I was looking through a scarcity lens. A lens that led me to choose maps of either/or and win/lose options for myself. This created the situation where my husband had to show up to my work to get my attention.

When I understood that, I chose to change my lens from a scarcity lens to an abundant lens. This led me to create and find maps that generated both/and and win/win/win options for myself. The result was having quality time with family and friends, plus a successful career. What I thought was required for success was based on the limitations of the lens I had been using. Choosing a different lens created possibility, freedom and joy in my life.

You can have the life you desire. The question to ask yourself is: Are you willing to be honest and responsible for making the changes to create it? You can do this!

Remember, the lens you use determines the maps you choose. So, choose wisely!

Kimberly Allain

Kimberly Allain is passionate about living purposefully. She has spent the last 20 years helping individuals and organizations uncover and embrace their passion, see their vision more clearly, and find effective, life-giving ways to realize those dreams. She believes that each of us has the ability to have the personal and professional life that we desire through knowing and operating as our best selves. Through this, we each find a greater sense of purpose, along with greater levels of energy, confidence, and joy.

She created Allain Solutions to provide coaching, consulting, and training services that support the growth and development of people and organizations to be their best. Happiness, success, and profitability are directly connected to our ability to draw forth the best from, with, and for each other. To move to the next level, we need to develop mastery in how to do that for ourselves and others.

She engages her clients to be courageous and assists them in accessing tools to help them actualize their goals.

When she is not focused on her business, you'll find her traveling with her husband to visit and connect with family and friends. During football season, you'll find her enthusiastically cheering for her New Orleans Saints. Life is to be fully lived! She is definitely committed to embracing it all!

Visit Kimberly's:
Website: https://www.allainsolutions.us
LinkedIn: https://www.linkedin.com/in/kimberlyallain/
Facebook: https://www.facebook.com/allainsolutions

Scan Me!

Remember

By Linda Lunden

"The more you love, the more you can love and the more intensely you love. Nor is there any limit on how many you can love."

~ Robert Heinlein

$\mathcal{R}$emember

By Linda Lunden

I have read ancient masters, mystics, religious leaders, philosophers, and consulted mentors, and all agree at some level that we come into this life with all knowledge and wisdom. The key is to REMEMBER! When we are born, we are connected to Source, God, Spirit, Universe, whatever your belief may be. As we grow, that memory, that feeling of being *one with all* fades and we spend our lifetime searching for and trying to remember and *feel* that connection.

If we came into life with total recall of our connection to all things, there would be no experiences to have and no lessons to be learned. I believe we choose the lessons we want to learn and that through our experiences and life choices, we have free will to learn and grow spiritually in this lifetime.

When I ponder events and decisions made in my life, I ask myself, "Why didn't I know?" or "How could I not know?" The thing is, I have made mistakes and questionable decisions because I DIDN'T KNOW WHAT I DIDN'T KNOW! If only I had known! If all choices and decisions were made with love in mind, all would have gone much more smoothly and unfolded in miraculous ways!

Love of self, love for others, love for the process, love for the lessons, love for the experience. Oh my! I would have walked through all things in life without fear or concern and with a smile on my face, trusting all would be shown to me through love. Who knows how much I did not know? It's so simple, yet we make it difficult.

So, in this moment – now – I can only write about what I know is truth for me *today*! What is up front and center is relationships. We navigate these from the time we are little with our family and playmates. Then we go to school and make friends and have crushes. When we graduate, we get jobs and have professional relationships. When romance appears, everything gets more complicated. Love and romance are the real teachers of self-love – where I believe the true lessons are learned and experienced.

Like everyone else, I have had my heart broken. There was a time when I told myself, "I am done with romance! How could he treat me this way?" But the truth is – how could I treat myself this way? No one can love me more than I love myself. If I don't speak up and say, "This is unacceptable behavior" – how would he know? How can I ask him to respect my feelings if I don't respect my feelings? Being understanding of behavior I don't like is just not honoring myself. Being vulnerable is being your authentic self and expressing it. When we have thoughts of, "I Want, I Need, I Miss" and so on, my feeling is that it's because we are not complete and whole within ourselves. *It is not the responsibility of anyone else to make us feel whole or loved.*

What a gift it is to just love someone. To feel a connection every time you see them. When your eyes meet, your heart smiles with that recognition of his inner soul. If that feeling is not mutual, then your heart embraces what is best for him… even if it is not you! From what I know today, that is true love!

It is important to remember:
"If your heart feels broken, you are feeling a need outside of yourself."

We are looking for the other person to satisfy a need to feel loved or desired. We want our feelings protected and understood. It must come from within ourselves. We are powerful and we create our own experiences.

It is important to remember:
*"If you miss him, it is that you have forgotten there
is no separation."*

We are all one, we are all connected. He is always with you, and you are always with him. Close your eyes and see him. Be mindful of carrying him in your heart.

It is important to remember:
*"If you feel the pain of separation, it is that you have
expectations in a love relationship."*

Whether it's the movies we have seen or observing other relationships, we expect love relationships to unfold in a certain way. Love can be so much more than we imagine. Trust it is perfect and all will be revealed in perfect timing and in a perfect way. Much, much more than we could have choreographed for ourselves.

It is important to remember:
*"When you feel loss, it is that you have an attachment
to what you desire in a relationship."*

When he does or says this – it means he loves me, wants me, desires me. If he doesn't, then your mind makes up stories instead of loving the experience and the development of the relationship. If you could allow it to unfold, it will be much more than you could imagine, even magical!

It is important to remember:
"To keep your heart open and stay in total trust."

You feel the connection for a reason. I personally don't believe in coincidences, but I do believe in destiny. That awareness of lifetimes together. Trust that destiny brought you together. Now you can choose to see the blessing or the lesson. Ask yourself, "What gift is this to me?", and "What does this show me about myself?" We are given free will, so once we recognize the connection, we can choose how we move forward within the relationship. Perhaps he is the reason you open to even more love with someone else. If you trust the process, it is revealed.

It is important to remember:
"It is total freedom to love when you can love without conditions."

It does not have to be marriage; it doesn't have to be forever – IT JUST IS. Grow, experience, and feel the joy and gifts of the present relationship. Be in gratitude as it unfolds.

It is important to remember:
"To love the "God-self" or God within and you will feel
"at-one-ment."

The Bible says, "Behold the kingdom of God is within you", that God's love is what connects us all. There is nothing missing. We do not need to look outside of ourselves to experience love.

It is important to remember:
"The power of love is when you love ALL things and ALL people."

Enjoy the beauty of nature and all its wonders. Be in awe of the total unconditional love animals have for us. We all have that light and love within. Acknowledge that spark within all that you encounter.

It is important to remember:
"To experience Divine Love means you need nothing in return. The
FEELING is complete."

Love as deeply as you feel. Love freely without fear. The outcome doesn't matter. There is no hurt or loss. You love no matter what. You give and receive, and it is just joy!

Love isn't supposed to hurt! Our job is to keep our mind and heart open. I AM a work in progress. The more I experience, the more I learn, **THE MORE I KNOW I DON'T KNOW**.

I crack myself up!

Linda Lunden

After much study, Linda Lunden discovered what kinds of physiological effects the vibrations of color can have on the physical body. She created a workbook for clients to better understand the power of these vibrations. Linda possesses an endless curiosity about life. She has traveled to many countries, including making spiritual journeys to Peru and Egypt. Her desire is to help and inspire women to fully embrace self-love and empowerment through relationships.

Linda can be reached at lklunden@yahoo.com.
Interior Designer
Certified Hypnotist
Reiki Master
DCA Certified Diamontologist
Certified Scuba Diver

Learning To Be Comfortable Just Being Me

By Lisa Beaucher

"Worthy now. Not if. Not when. We are worthy of love and belonging now. Right this minute. As is."

~ Brené Brown

Chapter 24

Learning To Be Comfortable Just Being Me

By Lisa Beaucher

I love the process of writing. It allows me the gift to better under-stand myself of where I've been, where I am presently and where I want to go. Writing also provides me with the gentle nudge to recall the things I've previously learned but have temporarily forgotten.

During the many years I've been on this planet, I have experi-enced incredible happiness, joy and love. I've been blessed to know so many kind and gentle people, and I hope this is true for you as well. I also know that life isn't always hearts and flowers. Learning to love ourselves for who we are is often not as easy as we would hope.

Self-acceptance can seem like a dirty word to those who have a hard time loving themselves. In our minds, there are so many exam-ples of why we are flawed. Of course, there is always a barrage of negative self-talk, the inner critic, that reinforces this belief. "I can't believe I just said that I'm such an idiot…" or "Oh God, I'm so stupid. I can never get anything right…"

In my mind, I was supposed to be perfect. I would take on everyone else's problems and make them my own. I felt the need to fix everything so nobody else would have to feel the pain of their own bad choices. I would "people please" while playing the hero. At other times I would embrace the role of the martyr. I would take on so much more then I could handle and eventually became resentful when others weren't doing anything to help their own circumstances. The anger would build up inside me and I would bury it deep down, fooling myself and leading others to believe that it didn't bother me. I would do anything to be loved and accepted by others.

When I started digging into my own self critic, I found it was filled with emptiness and the hollow echoes of past programming. My feelings of unworthiness and the depression that followed were constant companions. I had numbed my emotions so much with negative self-talk that I never realized how empty I had become. These buried feelings kept me hiding in the shadows with a dreadful fear of being noticed, singled out or worse, being rejected by others. I was so eager to please that I would disregard my own wants and needs so as to not hurt someone else's feelings or feel the sting of their disappointment in my choices.

I've learned that this self-critic has its roots in the beliefs we formed of ourselves growing up. Being harassed by the bullies in the school yard for being different or "uncool", disappointing my parents and teachers or the rejection from my siblings and friends, whether actual or imagined, all contributed to the feelings of unworthiness. I felt myself to be separate, an outsider and often feeling rejected.

For me, the first key to unlocking and exposing this shame filled voice in my head was being aware of its existence in the first place. Catching and confronting these sneaky little voices as they began to tear me down, especially when I was feeling incredibly vulnerable, has been paramount to my healing. The critic within that played the role of judge, jury and executioner, calling me out and shaming me over every mistake or faux pas, had to be relieved of its duties! The perceived role of my inner critic was to help me feel in control as a way of coping with my fear of not being good enough.

I remember many times when I was feeling quite fragile, my inner critic would spout a shame-fest reminding me of my unworthiness. This unrelenting voice in my head would win every battle. My options became quite limited as to how I could live in this world. It was at that point that I began to notice how mean and destructive this inner voice had become. I decided to take my first leap of faith by beginning to reach out for help, which in my world of having to be perfect was unheard of. This is when I started to learn, and I'm still learning, to accept myself for who I am. Faults and all. My mind has fought me at each and every turn. I would say change, it would say no. I would say I am love. It would say you are nothing. Through the wisdom and compassion of many healers, counselors and my guide I've been able to summon the courage, time and time again, to face my inner demons.

Coming to the understanding that by turning my awareness into my heart, I could allow my own self-compassion to flow within instead of criticism. It is only then that my self-loathing inner critic cannot survive. Every time I allow loving compassion to be my inner voice, I am opening up to more love and acceptance of who I really am.

To accelerate my healing, I had to begin the process of accepting my failures and flaws. I'm becoming the observer of the negative programming that rattles around in my brain thereby changing the script to loving acceptance, patience and understanding. I've started being kinder to myself and listening to my compassionate inner voice, which is something I usually reserved for everyone else. I have begun to honor my own wants and needs while learning to address and nurture my inner child. I've needed to be willing to address my fears and take small but constant steps towards overcoming them. This was a necessary element. I am learning to forgive myself for all of my self-imposed struggles and the ways I've let myself down. I'm learning to question everything that my mind whips up that is contrary to how I want to love myself.

So often I've wished I could just press the "Easy Button" and, voila, problem solved, bad feelings gone, peace within. If it were only that easy. This is a process for sure. Changing the programming in my head hasn't been easy for me. A combination of meditation, energy healings and an incredible amount of determination to continue to move forward have been key to working through my back log of brain minutia. Some days I'm the hero of my life and some days I still struggle. I've become better at picking myself up, dusting myself off and recognizing the beautiful new opportunities waiting for me. I've noticed that by nurturing myself and understanding what I'm needing in the moment, I am able to find that peace within.

I'm not the girl I once was. By opening up to self-love and acceptance, I am now creating the opportunity to have a life filled with joy. I'm taking off the masks one by one and learning to be comfortable just being me.

Lisa Beaucher

Lisa Beaucher is a native New Englander, born and raised in the Boston suburbs. After raising four children in the mountains of New Hampshire, she was diagnosed with stage 2 breast cancer at the age of 49. She knew it was time for a change. Through an international community of lightworkers with the Modern Mystery School, Lisa became a second step initiate and a Certified Life Activation Practitioner.

Within the Lineage of King Solomon, Lisa has explored the higher realms of consciousness as an adept Kabbalist through the Universal Kabbalah program. As a 2nd step adept initiate, she has a unique opportunity to connect to the Tree of Life in a profound way. While exploring and studying the Kabbalah, she opens up to a deeper understanding of the Self while accessing greater peace, joy, and abundance.

Lisa created Gentle Hearts Healing in 2017, offering clients Life Activation healing sessions and providing MAX Meditation gatherings. She has continued her studies and added additional healing modalities to help adults who have difficulty getting through life's challenges. She assists her clients with releasing buried emotions that impact their physical, mental, emotional, and spiritual health. Lisa is a certified practitioner Life Activations, Soma Sound Therapy, Emotional Freedom Technique (EFT), and a Reiki Master Teacher. She also provides Angel Readings, and as an ordained minister, she assists people through their grief.

Website: http://www.gentleheartshealing.net/
Email: gentleheartshealing@yahoo.com

Scan Me!

Peace Begins at Home

By Lisa Law

*"A peaceful home and a peaceful heart are within you, too.
If you let go and believe, you will find them."*

~ Lisa Law

Chapter 25

Peace Begins at Home

By Lisa Law

In 2007, my world shifted on its axis with the sudden death of my mother. It was hard on all of us. That year I turned 40 and my grandmother 90. The day of my mother's funeral, my grandmother fell and broke her pelvis. Her accident thrust me into an unexpected care-taking role.

My two children were young, and I was selling real estate in a down-turning market. Over the same period, my husband's grandfather, who was the patriarch of their family business, also passed away. His transition left a vacuum and more change within our family. The entire landscape of my life was overwhelming. I developed severe anxiety, depression, and back pain.

I found myself traveling back and forth from New Hampshire to Florida to help my grandmother. I can remember sitting on the plane many times, not knowing what was going to happen next. I felt very alone. But, in truth, I never really was.

While we were together, Grammie Myra and I spent hours reminiscing. She had been a flight instructor at an early landing strip in Rhode Island. She taught students from Brown University how to fly.

She worked her way up through banking when finance was a man's world. She traveled and was well loved by all who met her. Her greatest regret was that she hadn't attended college. A life-long learner, she took every continuing ed class the bank offered and shared that my graduating from Wellesley College was one of her proudest days.

As we spent time together, I came to appreciate her extraordinary life. However, she was a world-class worrier – a tendency that constantly kept her on edge. She pointed out my many strengths and the beautiful family life my husband and I had built. Like her, though, my anxiety and depression had been preventing me from appreciating it. Worrying was a family pattern. I knew that if I didn't change, I too would someday be in my nineties never having found inner peace. So, I set out to find it.

The first place I focused was on my relationship with my husband. We were taking our stress out on each other. Our bickering was bothering me. I picked up a Feng Shui book and flipped to the section on love and marriage. I went around our home and put happy pictures in every corner. The fighting stopped immediately!

I thought to myself, "Wow! That was amazing!" I was hooked. I delved deeper and deeper into Feng Shui. The more I worked within our home, the better and more peaceful I felt. I saw a positive shift happening in our family, too. We became happier and more content.

Then, one day, while walking through my basement I stopped and looked around. As I surveyed the piles, I saw things from every person that had been important to me. Most were no longer in my life. A light-bulb went off in my head. I was not only the keeper of our family's stuff – I was holding all that emotion, too. I knew in that moment I had to clear it out to further my healing.

Over the next six months, my husband and I went top to bottom through our home. We evaluated everything. We kept what felt supportive to the peaceful life we wanted to lead. We sold, donated, and gave away everything else. Our house felt and functioned so much better and so did we. The more and more that I let go, the lighter I felt.

People asked me, "Lisa. Have you lost weight?" And I'd say, "Yes! Tons and tons!"

By the end of our decluttering, my anxiety, depression, and back pain were gone! I was more balanced than I had ever been. I wanted to teach what I'd learned to others. The Western School of Feng Shui offered a practitioner training. I thought to myself, "I'd love to do that!" I heard a voice in my head say, "Nothing's stopping you. Go do it!" I smiled and said, "Ok! I will!" I could hear a chorus of angels singing, "Yah, she finally figured it out!"

A month later, I found myself flying to California. I walked into the classroom on the first day not knowing anyone, but immediately feeling at home. I'd found a whole group of spiritual people where I could share the deepest parts of me.

Up until that point, I had a whole secret spiritual life. Only my husband and sister knew that I practiced Feng Shui or could hear angels connecting with me (though my mom said as a child I talked about angels constantly). The training opened me up and helped me integrate even deeper into myself and my purpose. When I said "Yes" to helping others create peaceful homes and to create peace within their lifestyles, a most amazing path opened for me. Opportunities to learn, travel, grow, and teach just came to me.

About a year after my Feng Shui certification, I received an invitation to meet a friend's spiritual mentor. Each time I looked at the invite, an electric jolt shot through me. The day of the event, the invitation surfaced again. I picked it up and said, "Ok. Ok. I'll go!"

The evening included a free meditation. I liked it so much I stayed for the weeklong program. During that week, I experienced a profound healing around my mother's passing and all that came after it. My intuitive gifts opened even more, and I had the opportunity to travel with an international group to Nepal for a meditation retreat.

Two weeks later, I found myself on an airplane jetting off again into the unknown. As the plane barreled down the runway and lifted into the air, I cried. I could feel my mother and grandmother sitting next to me cheering me on. I felt so much love and appreciation for my family and for all the ways I'd changed. I pondered, "If I hadn't spent all that time traveling to my grandmother's, would I have been brave enough to pursue Feng Shui or set off to the Himalayas?" I knew that everything had been preparing me for this moment.

I would go on to travel around the world many times. My letting go and saying, "Yes" brought me to India, Thailand, Bali, China, Peru, Chile, Europe, and across the U.S. to study everything from meditation to metaphysics. I was introduced to many cultures, many masters, and many healing techniques. A sense of tranquility settled in and has remained.

I set out to find inner peace and change a pattern within myself. I decluttered everything that worked against it and stepped into my mission. Over the last ten years, I've enjoyed sharing the benefits of Feng Shui, living a balanced lifestyle, and embracing my spirituality. I feel lucky to teach, consult, and write internationally. It's been an amazing journey.

Thank you to the Silver Sisters for this opportunity to share. I hope that I have inspired you. A peaceful home and a peaceful heart are within you, too. If you let go and believe, you will find them. Please reach out to me if I can help.

Lisa Law

Lisa Law is a well-respected consultant, writer, and speaker on Feng Shui, decluttering, and living a balanced lifestyle. She is a member of the International Feng Shui Guild and is a trainer and mentor for the Western School of Feng Shui. She has taught and consulted across the United States and Asia.

Bringing together the best of Eastern and Western healing traditions, Lisa delights audiences with her peaceful, down-to-earth teaching style. Lisa has been working in people's homes for the last 17 years, first as a realtor and now as a professional Feng Shui and design consultant. She established her Feng Shui business in 2011.

Her services include home consultations, staging, color consulting, Bagua readings, and decorating. She loves creating harmonious, high-functioning homes! Lisa is also a wellness trainer for businesses of all sizes. She hosts workshops, retreats, corporate programs, spiritual "lunch and learns," and The Western School of Feng Shui's Essential Feng Shui® Certification in Nashua, New Hampshire.

In 2015, she published *"Feng Shui Inspiration Cards and Guidebook: Create Positive Energy in Your Home and Lifestyle,"* which helps readers combine Feng Shui with setting intentions (available at www.LisaLawFengShui.com). She has contributed to spiritual publications and books on memory, the history of skiing, and spiritual mastery. A New Hampshire native, Lisa Law grew up at her family's ski area. She attributes her calm demeanor to being raised slop-side in rural N.H., as well as her spiritual travels, Feng Shui, and mindfulness practices. She is excited to participate in this book on wisdom!

Contact information:
www.LisaLawFengShui.com
http://www.LisaLawFengShui.com/blog/
http://www.Facebook.com/LisaLawFengShui/

Scan Me!

A Peony Withered on My Tenth Birthday

By Lulu Gao

"A rose is a rose is a rose is a rose."

~ Gertrude Stein, "Sacred Emily"

Chapter 26

A Peony Withered on My Tenth Birthday

By Lulu Gao

Until I turned ten years old, my life was filled with my parents' nagging, drawing, homework piled mountains high, and reading my favorite detective novels. Nothing was that exciting. I often loved to read Sherlock Homes and Agatha Christie. Don't ask me how I got those PG-13 books in China; as a sneakily smart girl who was raised up in a conservative family, I naturally got my way. I would read these books in a quiet corner and sink my mind into a thrilling world. In that world and only in that world, I could be an incredible intellectual who could solve all those tricky mysteries and be a hero who could lay to rest the victim's soul and comfort the victim's family. Abruptly, a brutal murder came to my ten-year-old life.

I still remember the day I found the body – it was my tenth birthday. It was a typical Friday, and I was ready to have happy hour with my friends as my regular Friday after-school routine. Just kidding! After school, I rushed home because I expected my mother was preparing to treat me to a feast to celebrate my birthday! My old home was on the fourth floor of the building. I smelled delicious cooking from the first floor, but the smell stopped on the third floor. My heart fell from the moon down to the earth. Crap! My mom must have forgotten my birthday, and she wasn't home yet! Crap again! I forgot my house key! What a birthday!

At least we had two other families who lived on the same floor. One of them could let me in and wait for my parents to get home. I skipped the family next to us because I overheard the couple who lived there had a huge fight the other night, and I wasn't sure if it was a good idea to walk into what we call a "mad fog." Unfortunately, the other family wasn't home. So, I had to knock on the "mad fog" door. I knew Miss Peony must be home because she was a housewife, and she was always home, either polishing her nails red or arguing with her husband over some guys who had bought her new gifts. Why did I call her Miss Peony? I think that my mother planted that impression in my mind. Once upon a time, my mother said, "The next-door lady's beauty is as stunning as a blooming peony." I couldn't agree more. Miss Peony had very fair skin and always wore red, which made her eyes look like black pearls shining on jade. She had long, curled black hair that always reminded me of Esmeralda in "The Hunchback of Notre Dame." I believe she is a Chinese Esmeralda. She always wore a bright smile and talked in a sassy way like she never cared about what rumors people were spreading about her. I admired that she had a dramatic life and lived in a way she liked.

Back to my birthday. I knocked on Miss Peony's door. Surprisingly, the door was already opened just a bit. I asked, "Miss Peony, I forgot to bring my key. May I come in and wait here?" No answer. I tentatively pushed the door a little bit, "Is anybody home?" The air was strangely quiet. I knew Miss Peony had a big fight with her husband the other night, but I didn't think Miss Peony would be too sad to forget to close the door. In fact, I don't think she cared about her husband that much. Their marriage was on the edge, according to one nosy lady who kept tabs on all her neighbors and knew everything that happened outside of her house: namely, my mom! Miss Peony was never that quiet. Her home always had music or the TV on. She couldn't stand being quiet alone at home. My curiosity encouraged me to walk inside the house to discover what was going on with Miss Peony.

I found a woman lying on the floor on her belly in a very twisted position. A sharp, scary feeling rapidly creeped from my head to toes and I was frozen there for a couple of seconds. Soon, I looked behind me. Maybe my detective instinct instructed me to do so to make sure the murderer had run away. I didn't know what drove my 10-year-old brain. I wasn't screaming like a normal kid. All I knew was I should see if she was dead. I held my breath and walked to her on tiptoes, which could save me steps and not disturb the police's forensicwork. I reached my fingers to the left side of her neck. No pulse. Maybe I got the wrong side? I didn't learn which side of the neck to take a pulse in elementary school! Nor did I learn it from reading Sherlock Homes! I tried on her right side of her neck, and I put my fingers under her nose to test her breath. Nothing happened. It was just as quiet as the rest of the house. I was too scared to turn her body around to check if there were any wounds. Thank God, I didn't do it – I wouldn't want to interfere in the forensics! I stepped back, but I couldn't see her face. Suddenly, sorrow came to my heart. I felt sorry that a beautiful peony was withered. The moment I walked out the door, I told Miss Peony, "I like you, and you were nice to me."

I closed the front door and tied the doorknob tightly with my Little Octobrist Red Scarf. I believed this would prevent someone else from sneaking into the house and disturbing the crime scene while I was out looking for help. I went to a convenience store down the street and called the police. While I was sitting by Miss Peony's door and waiting for them to arrive, my mom got home. I ran to her, hugged her, and couldn't help bursting into tears. "Something horrible happened to Miss Peony! Don't open that door!" I cried to my mom. She didn't believe me and wanted to open the door to check on Miss Peony. I held my mom tightly to not let her go inside. Maybe, in my 10-year-old mind, not letting her see was the only way to protect my mom from the fear and sorrow. The police came and went, the husband showed up without tears. Later that year, the murderer was caught. It was one of Miss Peony's "boyfriends." I saw this "boyfriend" sneak around here several times, and I would never forget his shifty eyes.

Since then, I have stopped dreaming about becoming a murder detective. That pretty peony in my heart withered when she was thirty-three years old. Now at age thirty-three, I wish I could tell her and that she could hear, "Miss Peony, I don't care what goes through the grapevine about you. You were a good person, you were always nice to me, and I like you."

Beauty fades, but memories of kindness live on.

Lulu Gao

Lulu Gao is a Chinese girl who grew up on the East Coast of China and now lives in Seattle with her nerdy but humorous husband Brandon and loud rabbit-chasing-but-never-catching furry son Murphy.

Lulu loves reading, movies, traveling, cooking and plans to start a YouTube channel to share her daily cooking. She currently is a full-time private chef to her husband.

The Productive Pause Invitation: Is it Waiting for You?

By Rev. Maggie Mongan

"Slow down to accelerate."

~ Rev. Maggie Mongan, CEO

Chapter 27

The Productive Pause Invitation: Is it Waiting for You?

By Rev. Maggie Mongan

As the alarm went off at 5:30 am, Theresa woke up disoriented. She was in a daze. Something was off – Theresa was in her bedroom and bumping into things. It was as if she had a massive hangover, but she hadn't been drinking. "What's wrong?" As she put her hand on the wall to keep herself from falling, she thought, "I don't know what's happening here. Something isn't right."

Theresa was discombobulated, but the kids needed to get ready for school now, or they'd be late. She staggered as she knocked on their bedroom doors to wake them. Then, she bumbled her way to the bathroom to prepare for the workday. While showering, Theresa was trying to understand why everything was *off* this morning. Nothing was unusual; yet, something was.

Throughout her day, Theresa was puzzled. She was very active but not present. She had this nagging dissatisfaction as if her day was living in a hazed environment. Plenty was happening, but there was a disconnect. Nothing seemed direct. There wasn't clarity. She was muddling through the day.

After dinner was complete, the kids left the table to play. Theresa sat there staring at a small floral bouquet her son had picked for her. As she gazed at the intricacy of each flower, a tear slid down her face. As other tears followed, she noticed her breathing had changed. It was deep and slow. "What's happening? Where did my dreams go? Why am I not happy?" she thought to herself.

As Theresa contemplated, another wave of thoughts appeared, "I did everything right. I did what everyone said I needed to do to be successful, but why don't I feel happy? I'm so busy doing, and I'm not enjoying my life and children as I had intended." Then, as Theresa sighed in frustration, she heard herself say, "Something needs to change."

Please slow down and re-read the above sentence. Theresa was at a decisive moment. It was Theresa's moment to discern. She felt like she had been in a deep sleep – as if she was living her whole life as a character in a dream.

Theresa realized she had a choice to make about how she was going to live her life. She had to make new choices to support what would bring her peace, love, joy, and hope. It was her moment to choose wisely.

Unknowingly, Theresa was experiencing her golden invitation. Every human experiences this, sometimes even multiple times throughout their life. I call this *The Productive Pause Invitation*.

Oversimplified, *The Productive Pause Invitation* is when you have a moment to change the trajectory you were on for the moment, the day, or your lifetime. This invitation isn't a sit in the corner and start drooling moment, even though it may begin this way. Instead, it is more of a hit the pause button to actively explore and discern what may serve you, and your loved ones, the best.

As you know, life can be very messy at times. Life will throw you twists, requiring you to make turns. You probably have experienced this in your life; however, better outcomes are achieved by responding instead of reacting. Reaction is a natural reflex, or an impulse, and unconscious action. Your reaction provides you action or activates the following steps to appear.

Responding is conscious action or being mindful to determine which steps will best support you. In this context, responding focuses on you choosing your experience. When you slow down to determine or discern what will serve you best, you accelerate your experience.

Typically, this creates better outcomes for you because you didn't react. Instead, you make time to consider possibilities by exploring options. This invitation requires you to take action (productive) to discern what's best during your pause (time out).

When you choose to accept *The Productive Pause Invitation*, you actively move from messy and out of control, perhaps even victim experience, to owning your experiences and taking control of what happens next. Undeniably, this can be messy and even a bit scary! What's the difference? You are in control. Yes, you control what is occurring. You are self-managing.

Yes, it is possible to self-manage better outcomes. It is possible to even self-lead. Self-management is about your habits, actions, and your mindset. Self-leadership is about envisioning (mentally picturing the future).

Self-leadership is essential to your evolution. You evolve by seeing possibilities and then choosing which opportunities you choose to live into next.

Self-management tends to be easier for most people to do than self-leadership. Why? Self-management is about doing. Self-leadership is about being. Even though we are called human beings, a vast majority of us are human doings. So we get caught in the doing of life. Then we ask, "Why am I so stressed, overwhelmed, exhausted, and unfulfilled?"

Remember our character, Theresa? She was unfulfilled. Could you relate to some part of her story? Sure! We have all been there – probably more than once. This is the process of one's evolution. It begins with the ugh. We become disheartened. Consciously or unconsciously, we stop.

CLUE: If you are stuck, it's probably because you are not consciously nor intentionally taking appropriate action. *The Productive Pause Invitation* is your friend and resolution.

Are there more steps and more techniques to effectively and efficiently move through this process? Yes, and our focus now is to prompt you to become aware of when you are experiencing your invitation for a productive pause.

Now that you are aware of this opportunity to self-lead yourself with *Right Thought*s and support yourself with *Right Actions* to fulfill your vision, you will begin to notice more opportunities for you to command your life and career with authority. You will start directing much more of what you experience and learn how to engage more favorably with your experiences than you are currently. You may even notice how each day provides you an opportunity to live from a position of being empowered.

I know this part may be challenging to see right now; however, I assure you empowerment is the beautiful byproduct of taking time to be.

Throughout life, we have moments of evolution. From becoming an infant to an adult, we evolve through each phase of life. Unfortunately, humans are constantly hurrying – trying to accomplish as much as possible. This prevalent approach is exhausting and leaves us feeling inadequate and unfulfilled.

Today, I invite you to walk a different path – the one *you* choose. But, of course, you have already been invited to do so.

The question is: Will you allow yourself to move from your prescribed fate to your chosen destiny?

Beginning now, you can alter the trajectory of your life. But, it does require a new way of thinking and behaving.

The Productive Pause Invitation is waiting for your R.S.V.P.

Why wait longer than necessary? Say, "YES!" and allow yourself to lead yourself to whatever makes your heart smile.

Rev. Maggie Mongan

Rev. Maggie Mongan is a Small Business Thought Leader, Master Business Coach & Strategist, and #1 International Bestselling Business Author. She's worked with Fortune 50 companies to solo-entrepreneurs. Additionally, she is commonly known for being the #1 Bestselling Book Series creator of "Brilliant Breakthroughs for the Small Business Owner – Vol 1-4," with Volume 5 releasing November 2021. Maggie believes we each have a message to share, which ultimately guides others. She shares her messages as a Community Builder, Speaker, Blogger & Author, and Course & Content Creator.

Almost 20 years ago, Maggie founded Brilliant Breakthroughs Inc., a coaching practice to holistically guide and simplify YOUR Business Brilliance. Additionally, she guides her clients to become marketplace leaders. Maggie's known for her simplified systems and marketing prowess, which helps businesses create profit and peace simultaneously. She's also a peace advocate who co-created a mobile app to help others generate peace.

Born a Wisconsinite, Maggie is a cheese lover, Harley rider, and stargazer. She's still madly in love with her husband of almost 40 years. But, perhaps, most noteworthy: Maggie created and published her #1 Bestselling Book Series for Small Businesses while recovering from not 1, but 2, severe Traumatic Brain Injuries!

Website: https://www.BrilliantBreakthroughs.com
LinkedIn: https://www.linkedin.com/in/MaggieMongan
Mobile App: Brilliant Biz Book (Small Business Support)
Mobile App: Generating Peace
Author Profile: https://amazon.com/author/maggiemongan

Scan Me!

Turn Off Stress, Turn On Joy

By Marie Fowler

"I have lived in the pursuit of a vision: to care for what is noble, beautiful, gentle; where individuals grow freely, where hate, greed and envy die because there is nothing to nourish them."

~ Bertrand Russell

Chapter 28

Turn Off Stress, Turn On Joy

By Marie Fowler

What if there is a turn-off switch for stress? What if it is easy to learn, simple to use, and only takes a few minutes? What if results come quickly and last? What if it can be applied anytime, anywhere? What if it is free and evidence-based? How much would your life, health, and relationships improve?

Up to 90% of all doctor visits are for stress-related ailments and complaints. Add to that, the myriad of stressors the world has experienced since the start of the pandemic, and the need to learn how to turn off the stress response is at an all-time high. When we are overwhelmed by stress, it negatively impacts every aspect of our lives. Our sleep and eating habits become off. We become short-tempered in our relationships, tend to make poor choices, and struggle to get things done.

The physiological response to stress is called the fight or flight response, which occurs when we perceive that we are under excess pressure, and it is designed to protect us from harm and danger. Our sympathetic nervous system immediately engages in creating a cascade of physiological changes, pumping adrenaline into our system, increasing our blood pressure, heart, and breathing rate, all of which work to enable us to fight or flee from a stressful or dangerous situation. For many people, their nervous systems become stuck in chronic fight or flight mode, and the body and mind cannot fully heal when it is in this state.

The good news is that we CAN turn off the fight and flight response in our nervous system. Instead of being at the effect of stress, or the difficult and painful things that happened to us in the past, we can become free of their grip and operate more from choice, inspiration, and intuition. Harvard Medical School's Mind-Body Medicine Institute calls this eliciting the relaxation response which is a helpful way to turn off the fight-or-flight mechanism, bringing the body back to pre-stress levels. Research has shown that regular use of the relaxation response can help any health problem that is caused or exacerbated by chronic stress.

There are several methods that can elicit the relaxation response, and a new wave of evidence-based techniques has proven their effectiveness. The Emotional Freedom Techniques/EFT, aka tapping, quickly and powerfully delivers the benefits discussed in the opening paragraph and is the set of techniques that I most often teach clients and continue to utilize myself.

We all know when we are carrying too much stress in our bodies. We instinctively start rubbing our foreheads, neck, and shoulders to relieve stress and gain comfort. When we consciously and intentionally rub or tap on the acupressure points used in EFT, research shows this has an immediate calming effect on our nervous system, reducing the stress hormone cortisol, turning off the stress response, and turning on the relaxation response.

As a person with some of the characteristics of a type A personality, I developed chronic fatigue in my 20's and struggled with being "wired but tired." When a physician friend introduced me to these techniques, not only was I able to regain my health, but I became so much better at handling the slings and arrows of life.

I will never forget a young man who came to see me, who had been using recreational drugs to manage the PTSD flashbacks he was experiencing from a childhood trauma, which were starting to adversely affect his job performance. He described the memories like a full-color 3D movie always playing in his mind. After our session, he shared the memories became black and white and then completely faded in the distance. He shared that he is a "tool guy" but never had the tools to deal with PTSD before. Now that he had learned EFT, he was better equipped to manage life.

EFT tapping can also be used to help people attain peak performance, as both professional and Olympic athletes use this tool. When playing at such high levels, these athletes are already highly developed in their physical skill and prowess. What separates the winners from the losers is their mental game, how they handle loss, setbacks, and mistakes, which is why they use EFT. Business and sales professionals also utilize EFT to release any blocks to achieving their goals.

The other traumatic stressor that has risen dramatically since the pandemic, is violent hate crimes. We saw what happened to George Floyd, Jewish temples being desecrated, bills being written against the LGBTQ community, and Asians and Asian Americans around the world being scapegoated for the pandemic. EFT tapping can be highly effective in not only releasing the trauma from these events, but the secondary trauma from witnessing such acts, whether in person or in the media. There are also concrete actions we can take to create a better world at the societal level.

The U.S. Government has declared the rise in anti-Asian hate crimes at emergency crisis levels, rising by over 150% since the pandemic started, often leading to serious injury and sometimes death. As a woman of mixed race of both Filipino and Caucasian descent, I encourage everyone to help end all of this, by speaking out against every act of violence, and using your phone to record any incidences on camera. Please also consider supporting Asian-Americans running for political office who are committed to equality for everyone. Due to the work of Congresswoman Grace Meng in New York and others, the Anti-Asian Hate Crime bill was passed. She has also sponsored a bill to teach Asian American history in our school system, which you can ask your representatives to support.

I propose we all take a stand in supporting Justin Michael Williams vision and work to end all forms of racism in our lifetime. You can Google his writings and talks on this topic, find out more about the Liberation Experience, his book "Staying Woke" and other resources at: https://www.wecandreambigger.org.

Civil rights leader Valerie Kaur's work on revolutionary love and her book "See No Stranger," expands on the teachings of Gandhi, to address how we can care for ourselves by letting joy in. "Joy returns us to everything good, beautiful and worth fighting for. It is a revolutionary act, because it gives us energy for the labor. We will one day be someone's ancestors. If we get this right, they won't inherit our trauma, but our bravery, born of joy. I have come to believe that laboring for a more just and beautiful world, with love and with joy, is the meaning of life." Her website is https://www.valeriekaur.com.

EFT tapping and other methods I use and teach, truly support people in letting joy in, by letting stress, anxiety and trauma out of the nervous system for good. This empowers people to effectively deal with life's challenges, stop cycles of trauma, abuse and hate, allowing for higher levels in consciousness and contribution, to create a world that works for all. To immediately experience the benefits from this work and use EFT in your day-to-day life, begin by getting your free stress relief meditation at my website https://www.zoneofwellness.com

Marie Fowler

Marie Suzette Fowler MSW, is trained as a psychotherapist with a Masters Degree in Social Work, Direct Practice Counseling, with a specialization in Psychoneuroimmunology. She completed her internship at Banner Behavioral Health Hospital and several hundred hours of advanced training in the fields of holistic and mind-body medicine, from institutions that include Scripps Memorial Hospital in San Diego. She has studied and trained under the leading doctors and psychologists in these fields and is certified in a multitude of the most cutting-edge healing modalities available today. Marie is also a Board-Certified Holistic Healthcare Practitioner with 25 years of experience. She specializes in resolving stress-related conditions and helping clients overcome blocks to achieving their goals. Her background also includes training physicians in these techniques.

Marie's work is based upon the treatment of stress, which Harvard Medical School's Institute of Mind-Body Medicine has proven to be effective in resolving many health conditions. Her work is also based upon the principles of Traditional Chinese Medicine, which the National Institutes of Health has approved for the successful treatment of pain and other conditions.

Equally passionate about social justice, Marie founded a nonprofit that addressed the growing trend of wrongful convictions in the US and helped to free an innocent woman from death row. She also enjoys traveling, dancing, and playing with her niece and nephews.

Marie currently practices in Phoenix, Arizona, offering individual appointments and classes, in-person and online. For a free stress reduction meditation, visit her website: https://www.zoneofwellness.com

Scan Me!

Have You Ever Wondered?

By Marilyn Poscic

Dear Guys,
Please give me clearance to clarity for complete
understanding of
Your messages to obtain complete love, healing and
forgiveness of Your divine guidance.
Thank you!

~ Marilyn Poscic

Chapter 29

Have You Ever Wondered?

By Marilyn Poscic

As a child, what did you wonder about? Did you wonder what it would be like if your family had more or less money? Did you wonder about what you were going to be when you grow up, have imaginary playmates, hold parties with them, and wondered why you couldn't actually see them like you did everyone else? Have you ever looked into the sky or below the ground and wonder what's really there? Ever wonder what those clouds look like to you?

Growing up in the small town of Canton, Ohio, I wondered about so many things. I was the only protestant in an all-Catholic neighborhood. I wondered if I was really going to hell when I died because I was not a Catholic and confessed my sins. I wondered why you had to confess your sins to another person. Wasn't talking to God enough?

I loved watching westerns on TV and wondered what it would be like to live in that period of time (little did I know I did have a past life then)!

I wondered what it would be like to fly, to be popular and pretty in school and my most prevailing wonderment as a child was, I always wondered if I was adopted.

As I became an adult, I decided I wanted to be a stewardess. However, the requirements were very strict, and I could pass the eye test. So, I decided to get a profession in the medical field because deep down I knew one day I would move to a warmer place and wanted to be assured of a job!

My parents made me go to college even though I wondered why, but I knew they had my best interest at heart. Wondering what I was doing there other than too much partying, I searched for a medical profession that did not require a college degree and became an X-Ray technician for more than 20 years. All safe, good income, allowing me to move to AZ for the warmer climate, right? Still, I wondered. Why did I not feel happy, content, fulfilled?

Little did I know 15 years after moving to AZ my life would be turned upside down. My only sibling, my brother passed of Aids. I wondered what happens when we die. Is death really final? I had no reason to question death as it is an expected occurrence in life. I wondered if I was in denial of losing my only brother? I was given a few books to read about the afterlife, learning we don't really die. Our physical bodies die, but our spirit remains very much alive as I soon discovered a few years later when I began to see Angels and "dead" people around my friends and family and would relay the messages I received. Many felt it was wonderful while just as many thought I had lost my mind. These visions and messages became stronger, especially when I tried to ignore them.

A friend recommended taking a reiki class since the "dead" people were becoming quite annoying, and I wondered if I was losing my mind only to discover by my Reiki teacher that I was a very powerful healer, and all of these messages would become stronger. Although I wondered what this all truly meant, I proceeded to become a Reiki Master Teacher. It felt right! Instead of wondering about all the unknowns of what this meant, I decided to embrace it! I worked with many psychics, read books, and took classes. I adapted to this like a duck on water. (Now that I teach classes, I realize this is what I was meant to do as many have a difficult time learning as well as accepting), I was discovering my passion and fulfillment in life, even though I wondered what this all meant and what I was going to do with this new-found love.

I went from being an X-Tay technician to realtor, mainly because I absolutely did not like the medical field, and I wondered about the days when I would become a millionaire by selling real estate!

However, my "Angel" brain became stronger as word got out about my readings and people began to come to me for private sessions and having Angel parties. I truly wondered what this all meant and if I was good enough to have people pay me for my messages.

My world began to shatter. I got a divorce, my father, my rock, developed Alzheimer's, which we had to place in a home and watch him become a child, where he eventually passed away after being in the home for a year. Four years later, the whole world shattered when my mother, my last surviving relative, suffered a massive stroke in a casino and passed five months later! In a matter of 14 years, my life that I did truly enjoy was turned upside down. Now more than ever did I wonder, now what?

I was in a deep state of depression and didn't want to live anymore either. Why am I still here and all of my loved ones are not? Why them and not me? Oh, how I wondered.

Luckily for me, my Guys, which is the nickname I have assigned all the Angelic realm I work with, had other ideas. As I began to evolve out of my fog of depression and grief, I was guided by Them to write a book about my experiences of my mother's final 5 months of life, battling the insurance companies. I didn't even wonder if this book would make me a fortune. I knew with certainty it was a book to help others so they didn't have to go through exactly what I had to go through.

Life began to fall into place for me solely doing my spiritual work. I no longer wondered, why them not me. I know without a doubt that all of them had to pass in order for me to step fully forward to do my loving, fulling spiritual work! I began teaching classes, doing more Angel/Medium sessions, holding group meditations as well as writing two other books. My life began to be less and less of wonderment and more of fulfillment.

Do I still wonder about my life? Of course! I feel that is a human trait. However, I am proud to proclaim that the wonderment of life no longer holds a place of fear for me. When I question anything in my life, I have learned to ask the Guys for Their love, help, advice and truly listen and trust in my heart the messages I receive. I unquestionably can say, if I can do this, so can you.

When you begin to know, trust and understand the vastness of a world beyond our human knowledge, your life will change in miraculous ways you haven't even begun to imagine!

I now actively help others to stop wondering about their life and guide them on a path that the Angels can help us with no matter what without that constant nagging of fear and wonderment.

Marilyn Poscic

Marilyn Poscic is an Internationally known Intuitive Angel Messenger/ Medium and Author of *Last Soul Standing, Angels Simplified,* and her children's book, *Angels, Angels Everywhere* and has created eight meditation CD's who loves spending time out in nature, especially by the ocean or mountains, being around animals especially dogs and horses of which she has had many in her life and taking walks to really connect with her Guys!

Marilyn helps to reveal the lessons you are here to learn by expanding your awareness and recognition of your Angels and other Spiritual Guides you need for personal awareness, closure, and healing.

She assists thousands of people in finding their own spiritual guidance by connecting them to their inner truth, bringing comfort, closure, healing, and peace through messages from Angels and deceased loved ones in her private and group sessions, spiritual mentoring, spiritual classes, and meditations.

https://marilynposcic.com/
marilyn@marilynposcic.com
https://www.facebook.com/
angelmessengermarilynposcic

Scan Me!

Growing Wisdom

By Marlene Sabatina

*"It's by Grace, Love, and Caring
that a garden and relationships grow."*

~ Marlene Sabatina

Chapter 30

Growing Wisdom

By Marlene Sabatina

As a child, I grew up close to a family dairy farm in southern Vermont. From an early age, I had an innate connection with nature and an awareness of the changing season. Each new season brought new things to see and fresh excitement for me. I was infused with the connection of my grandparents; as we walked through the garden to harvest vegetables, it truly became a harvest of relationships of the family kind. I became aware of the annual cycle of life as we worked and strolled through the seasons, watching the bright spring colors emerge from the ground. I was especially delighted in the rather large patch of Lily of the Valley, such a delight to pick a huge bunch and present them as a gift. A gift from the heart by way of the garden!

My grandparents planted vast fields of crops for selling as well as cultivating a garden for their use. My summer memories are so fresh of my grandfather having bushels of corn for sale. So many customers came, and I know I gained the wisdom of how my grandfather interacted with each of them. Sometimes he would send me off to the strawberry fields. He liked me to pick because I was close to the ground, and I was fast. After picking baskets of those strawberries, we would sell them on the spot. Perhaps that is where I gained my entrepreneurial spirit.

My parents, although not farmers, still had a passion for cultivating their vegetables and herbs. In those days, produce was not readily available from the supermarket, so people were much more self-sufficient and connected to the land. However, I learned that they were very persnickety when it came to preparing and cooking those vegetables. They must always be fresh and cooked that day; farm to table is what it is referred to these days.

My mother also understood the beauty of flowers and their power to comfort and heal. She kept carefully tended flower beds close to the house, so there was always an uplifting view from each window. The vegetables nourished our bodies, and the flowers nourished our souls. Anyone who came by the house was always treated to a vase of flowers and yummy treats to eat. At the time, I did not fully appreciate what I was witnessing or the vast wealth of knowledge on display. I would take their careful attention to detail for granted and did not realize how profoundly affected I was by this silent nurturing until years later. Shortly after settling into my first home with my husband, I began my own journey of discovery as a novice gardener and planted raised flower beds but had no clue what I was doing. With my grandparents gone and my parents far away, I turned to the local professionals at the garden center for advice, who were only too willing to impart their knowledge.

In 1999, I had the privilege of owning a bed and breakfast in Nova Scotia, Canada. We arrived in early spring when flora and fauna were still dormant. I was unfamiliar with the local plants, so I sought advice from a Master Gardener in the area. She assessed the emerging plants, and together we mapped out the garden beds. Her expertise was invaluable and allowed me to move forward with my plans. Six months later, with much enthusiasm, I renovated the existing garden and created a lot more. Almost too much for one person to handle!

However, the results were beautiful, and I was honored by the local flower club to be included in their tour. All these endeavors reaped their own harvest for me as relationships, knowledge, and connections were built.

I am an artist and jeweler and work with precious metals extracted from the earth. The flowers and trees in my garden provide endless inspiration for my designs. Even when I am not gardening, the forms are alive in my imagination and encourage me to interpret their beauty in new ways and create objects of desire. Nature is an integral feature in our lives. Often, I have people stop by and want to know what plant this or that is in my garden. I am still seeking knowledge of the botanical names, but I often refer to them by common name.

We connect to flowers on an emotional level and often decorate our homes with beautiful blooms, the hand-picked endeavors from our gardens. We also offer them as gifts for an expression of love. Imagine a wedding or other event without flowers. Being a gardener is not just about textbook learning; it's about experience, empathy, and patience. Knowledge is acquired over time through trial and error, through small snippets of information from first-hand encounters with experts and mother nature. This slow accumulation of wisdom builds without noticing until we suddenly realize we know some of the answers.

The knowledge we have acquired converts to an instinctive response and provides awareness to others. I like to share my knowledge and experience with fellow enthusiasts and hope that some of my wisdom will filter down to future generations. As I see it, this also translates to relationships. Think about how to cultivate those special connections – increasing our knowledge of that person, where their journey took them, and why. Communication and gardening can create such beauty of their own kind.

In these times of instant gratification, it's easy to forget what great satisfaction can be derived from careful, patient nurturing, both in gardening and in our relationships. We can follow the manual, but experiences allow us to adapt and go with the flow if unusual or adverse conditions arise. Over the years, I have learned a lot about cultivating plants, and I like to apply what they have taught me to my personal relationships.

Growing from a seed into a beautiful plant is not always the straightforward process the textbooks would have you believe. Adverse conditions can hinder growth. Unexpected frost or too much sun, drought or too much rain, hard clay or sandy soil; the conditions need to be just right for the plant to reach its full potential, and I do all I can to help it along the way. In the same way, I intuit what my family and friends need to help them prosper, and I am always there to offer my love and support.

In my garden, there is space for everything and everyone. Each plant and flower and tree, all so different. Standing alone, they may not look like much, but when I bring them together and provide the right conditions, they flourish and reward all who see them with their intense beauty. Stop by sometime and we will share our wisdom together.

Marlene Sabatina

Marlene has been an entrepreneur for many years. Having worked as a secretary in the medical field for many years. She wanted to move on to express her creative flare and started her own retail clothing and accessory shop, Marlene's Fashion Experience. Working in retail created many avenues that lead to other endeavors.

Marlene created a tea business where she served "high" tea at various home functions. She took classes as a "chef enthusiast" and still caters when requests come her way.

Marlene was trained in Feng Shui and used this knowledge for Interior Decorating with a desire for beautiful spaces and further creative expression.

Nature's Cottage Bed & Breakfast was established in 1999 in Nova Scotia, Canada, and was noted in Frommer's publication after only a few years in business.

While in the retail business, she discovered a love of metalsmith jewelry, and that drew her to study under many talented jewelry teachers over the past several years. Being drawn to the mixed metals, she started to master this diverse form of Art. She established her studio, Feather Heart Studio, where she creates one-of-a-kind jewelry. Her love of sharing nature and inspiration has led her to offer classes also.

She has shown in several gallery settings around the Phoenix/ Scottsdale area and has exhibited across the country in art shows.

Marlene Sabatina
Feather Heart Studio
602-919-9233
Cave Creek, Arizona
www.featherheartstudio.com

My Holistic Journey to Healing After Great Loss

By Mary Kay Owen

"Sometimes you have to let go of the picture of what you thought life would be like and learn to find joy in the story you are already living."

~ Rachel Marie Martin

Chapter 31

My Holistic Journey to Healing After Great Loss

By Mary Kay Owen

Our son and daughter, Preston and Jena, were only 13 and 7 respectively when their father died. Nothing can prepare you for that shock. Our hearts were broken, and nothing could ever fill the void of our loss. It was hard getting from one day to the next. How could God take their Father? I felt like God took the wrong parent. Jon was so loving, kind, and gentle. Never in a hurry, he always had time to play. I couldn't possibly fill his shoes.

No one should lose their father when they're so young and my heart ached for my children. My whole life's focus changed when Jon died. I wanted to talk with him and have him help me with our children. I started to do whatever I could to connect with Jon again.

One of the first signs that Jon was around occurred after Jena found out her dad had died. She cried until she cried herself to sleep. When she woke up, the first thing she said was, "Everything is going to be alright." She was only 7. How could she possibly know that? Once, when Preston was crying inconsolably, he looked up to the corner of the room. I know in my heart that he had a vision of Jon because his crying stopped for no apparent reason. I was so filled with grief that I felt the only person who could help me find peace was Jon. I looked for ways to communicate with him.

One day after a meeting, I was driving and noticed a sign for the grand opening of a new spa. I felt compelled to turn my car around and go inside without understanding why. When I walked in, a lady came out of an office. Once I saw her, I knew she was the reason I was there.

She was a clairvoyant, so I asked if she had some time. "Yes. I have an hour that just opened up." She felt Jon's spirit immediately. She told me how sad he was to have left us, but that he was where he needed to be. She knew about my children through what Jon told her from the other side. He said he was always with us and always watching out for us. There were many things she told me that only Jon could know, so I had no doubts that Jon was speaking directly to me.

I believe we're guided to do things we wouldn't normally think of, like the day I stopped at the spa. The messages from Jon meant so much to me and validated that he was in a good place. I felt reassured that he was continuing to help me with our children, and he was doing everything he could to protect them.

That day at the spa was a major turning point for me. It was the beginning of a healing journey so that I could cope with raising my children. I felt immeasurable pain from the loss of Jon and my children suffered so much. I know I wasn't really present for them during the first few years after Jon's death because of my own despair. I looked for ways to find peace so that I could be a better parent and try to find happiness again.

I started to meditate, which gave me peace. I actually felt like I connected to Jon's love during those moments. In my mind, I talked with him and knew he understood everything I said. *I would get a sense of peace that only came during meditation, so meditating became very important. It's a practice that I continue to this day.*

About this same time, I became very curious about Reiki, which is a form of energy healing. I took a few classes, but the most interesting part was that whenever a Reiki master did Reiki on me, my loved ones would show up. I felt their presence and love. It was a miracle to have those connections.

There are many gifted people in the world who connect with those on the other side, so I sought out various individuals. Once, I phoned a shaman who was recommended, and that phone consultation was life changing. She felt the ball of grief that I had been carrying for years. She took me on a journey to leave that ball of grief behind. Jon wanted me to be happy and his love for his children was as strong as ever. It was extremely difficult to let go of the grief I was holding onto. When she finally convinced me to let it go, I felt lighter, like a significant weight was lifted. It was a very special gift.

We can heal our hearts with the help of others, and I was fortunate that I could seek out help in various ways. I have had spirit flights, wisdom circles, counseling, and wonderful friends to see me through hardships in life. Not everyone reaches out to heal their hearts, so that's why I felt compelled to tell my story – to let others know that there are ways to feel better and make peace with devastating loss. Life will never be the same, but you can get through it and find new ways of living with more joy.

Through tragedy, I found my connection with God. I look to God for answers during troubling times and always feel His presence. I feel a genuine peace, which can only come from God. I feel His healing white light surrounding me when I call out to Him. God is always with me, especially during deep meditation.

You feel like you don't deserve to be happy when someone you love dies, but I know that all they want is for us to be happy. Love is eternal and continues beyond the grave. Love is the only thing that is real and cannot be taken away from us. Love is a gift to be cherished and never taken for granted.

Everyone has lessons to learn in life. One of my biggest lessons was learning how to forgive myself for things I thought I did wrong. I'm a work in progress. I have found that connecting with God, meditating, taking care of myself and surrounding myself with positive, like-minded people are great ways to find peace and joy.

We tend to withdraw when we're unhappy but connecting with others is a magical way of healing. I believe we all want to be of service to others. Having deep relationships heals my soul.

Over the years, I have continued my studies of Reiki, meditation, and shamanic healing. I am certified in teaching meditation and mindfulness. I also became a Reiki master and a shamanic breathwork facilitator because I have experienced the value of these healing modalities and want to share them with others.

It's often said that everything happens for a reason. We don't always know what that reason is. Losing Jon put me on the path to healing deep wounds which ultimately redefined my purpose. I know now that I am here to serve others who have wounds to heal. That is my soul's purpose.

Mary Kay Owen

Mary Kay Owen enjoyed a successful career in the travel industry for over 25 years in the state of Nevada. Her love for travel and learning about other cultures inspired her to visit 53 countries on five continents.

Throughout her life, Mary Kay has experienced great love and great loss. After losing her first husband, father and grandfather, she embarked on a healing journey of self-discovery in which meditation, Reiki and breathwork were key components. Experiencing the healing benefits of these holistic modalities as well as a variety of spiritual practices that she gleaned all over the world she knew she wanted to share these gifts.

Mary Kay then became a certified Reiki Master, a certified meditation teacher and a breathwork facilitator so that she could share her knowledge with others.

Mary Kay is a heart-centered trail blazer and enjoys connecting with groups and individuals. Her non-judgmental approach puts others at ease, helping them feel peaceful and safe. Mary Kay motivates and inspires individuals to be the very best they can be. With heartfelt gratitude for others, she recognizes her gift to guide transformational change through support, compassion and unconditional love.

Mary Kay is extremely passionate, committed to making a difference and is striving to help make the world a better place. She now offers meditation, Reiki and intuitive counseling at Owen Meditation Center ("OMC") in Scottsdale, Arizona.

Connect with her to be guided into a practice that can transform your life.

marykayo2011@gmail.com

Facebook: Mary Kay Owen

Instagram: marykayowen

Scan Me!

Surrender to the Tiger

By Melissa Myers

*"If you keep your heart open through everything,
your pain can become your greatest ally in your life's
search for love and wisdom.*

~ Rumi

Chapter 32

Surrender to the Tiger

By Melissa Myers

Wisdom is within us all. It is related to our Essence, the part of us connected to Source. Perhaps it is the bridge between our Humanity and Divinity. It is formed by moving through our conditioning, heartbreaks, trials, and tribulations… using it all as "grist for the mill," as they say. Wisdom is developed through a life truly lived as we begin to see past the surface of what is occurring and cultivate the ability to look deeper, beyond the illusion. Wisdom is not the same as knowledge and cannot be obtained through a book or class but rather from raw, unbound life experience; oftentimes the ones that push you to your limit. It is earned in those moments where we rise from the ashes of yet another devasting opportunity to accept and integrate the deeper truths and meaning of this tragically beautiful life-death cycle. It requires us to fully experience change and loss, surrender to it, and allow it to bring us to a truer version of who we are.

Fifteen years ago, I went through one of the first major waves of change and loss of my life, which included the death of both of my fathers and 7-year relationship with my partner as well as the projects/dreams that mattered most to me. As a result, I was guided to leave the U.S. on a journey that would shake my very being to its core and in bumpy, messy jolts and stumbles, begin to awaken my inner wise woman. All that had defined who I was and given me the relative sense of safety that most of us hide behind for protection, had crumbled. Those waves would crash against my World many more times along the way.

The more death visited in all its many shapes and forms, the faster I ran, harder I worked, tighter I grasped, and the more I suffered. So much effort and energy wasted trying to protect myself from further pain and loss. Meanwhile, I reluctantly yet earnestly tried to tap into and follow the whispers of my soul and finally started to tend to the whimpers of the frightened little girl within. Perhaps that was precisely what I had set off to do in the first place. Maybe it's we all came here for.

During my first year of training at the Transpersonal School, a Buddhist monk told me something that changed my perspective and life forever. He said, "Surrender to the Tiger".

Letting go has never come easily to me. I am a survivor. I fight, hang on for dear life, even when my nails are ripping from my fingertips as I hang from the ledge. But the Greater Wisdom that moves the Universe has continuously pushed me over that edge while, at the same time, catching me and gently guiding me back down to solid ground. I am slowly learning to trust it and to discern when to hold on and when to let go, as well as how to do both simultaneously.

Change, loss, and death are inevitable and necessary parts of Life. They are not problems to be overcome, but fundamental parts of our experience on this planet. They are opportunities for growth, depth, and awakening. They are our greatest teachers. There is absolutely no one who doesn't have to face them sooner or later. The question is, how do we face them? As victims of circumstance and a cruel World or God? Or do we embrace them?

Embracing them means we open our hearts wide enough to hold all of it. It means we allow what is to be, give space to our feelings, honor the process, and practice again and again the art of letting go.

We experience many forms of death throughout our lives. Buddhist teachings remind us of impermanence; everything changes. From break-ups and divorce, to losing our job, our health, our dreams, loved ones, and eventually, our bodies.

And yes, it hurts. It hurts to say goodbye. It hurts to let go. Yet it hurts even more to oppose what is. Khalil Gibran says, "…For life and death are one, even as the river and the sea are one." When we resist death, we resist life. If we don't fully open to death, we cannot fully open to life.

When we are able to keep our hearts open, we experience the beauty, tenderness, and wonder of this precious, fleeting life. We feel a sense of gratitude and trust, even in the face of change and loss. When we keep our hearts open, we see beyond the surface to deeper truths that our minds alone simply cannot fathom. We discover a kind of timeless, formless, limitless love that is our very Essence.

Our tendency is to close, to try to protect ourselves... it is part of our wiring to do so. As we pay attention with kindness, practice inward listening, and hold space, we bring love to our vulnerability, and connect with our inner strength.

Goodbyes are some of the most excruciating moments of our journey and yet, perhaps, right there within that pain is the very tender ache that leads us back to Source.

I am fortunate to have amazing women in my life who have been examples of this open-hearted wisdom. My Grandmother, Marjorie Myers, just turned 103. She has lived through more heartbreak, change, and loss than anyone I know. And what I admire most is her incredibly bright shining open heart. When she is gone wisdom reminds me that she and I will forever be united in that shared space.

Our open, awakened hearts have room for everything... for the greatest joys and the deepest sorrows. Nothing is excluded from this sacred space. Although we may feel afraid; afraid to feel pain, afraid to let go, afraid to open... our heart has the capacity to hold the fear and the grief. As we courageously allow it to move through us, we encounter our inner gifts, freedom, and wisdom. When we surrender to the tiger, in all its varying forms, it becomes our ally, and we reclaim our lives.

Great Belly of Existence

Even in the darkest hours, there are infinite points of light.
Sometimes like glints of hope they come through the kind words of a friend,
Or the sound of the birds singing outside the window.
Even when the shades are pulled all the way down,
And darkness fills the room,
Sometimes just their persistent melody guides us toward the light.
Those long, dark nights when our fears grip us in the blackness,
A single ray of moonlight pierces its way through and reminds us we are not alone.
And when no light appears from outside
and the world itself seems to have been swallowed whole,
If we allow ourselves to be digested and integrated into the Great Belly of Existence,
Perhaps we discover that the Universe with its eternal darkness and infinite light,
reaching across all the dimensions of time and space, forms of life and death,
has always been within us, every step of the way.
Every laugh, every tear
Every triumph, every fear.
Intrinsically, inevitably, and undeniably intertwined.

~ Melissa Myers

Melissa Myers

Melissa Myers is a certified Transpersonal Psychotherapist, Life Coach, Spiritual Counselor, Reverend, Reiki Master, and Yoga/Mindfulness Instructor with a degree in Communications. She has been working with clients through a private practice since 2012.

She is a published poet and author of the journal, *The Path Part 1, The Inner Journey*, and the E-book *Breakthrough Crisis*.

For the past 15 years, she has lived in a small village in the Gredos Mountains of Spain, just a couple of hours from Madrid.

Melissa is the founding director of Relax in English LLC, offering retreat-style English Immersion Courses to Spanish business leaders based on Mindfulness and Emotional Intelligence. She has more than 20 years of experience organizing and imparting retreats, workshops, and various events.

Her path led her through many experiences and challenges/opportunities that contributed to awakening an intense interest in the human condition from a very young age. Her curiosity to understand life and humanity on a deeper level and deep connection with nature and Spirit has been her greatest inspiration. Melissa is a survivor of childhood trauma, including sexual abuse and bullying, and continues her healing journey facing, learning from, and bringing love to the resulting CPTSD and Erythrophobia.

Email: melissa.myers77@hotmail.com

Websites:
www.relaxinenglish.com
www.breakthrucrisis.com

Scan Me!

Traveler

By Nicoleta Taylor

"Say what Love would say, do what Love would do."

~ András Kovács-Magyar

Chapter 33

Traveler

By Nicoleta Taylor

There is this breathtakingly beautiful world called Earth, a neighbor with Venus and Mars, in the realm of the Sun. Its inhabitants come in many embodiments, all travelers throughout the creations of the Source.

This is my story of being a traveler who, just like you, has visited this world many lifetimes through the portals of birth and death. I am a spirit, a manifestation of Source in a certain stage of evolution. My essence is light energy carrying information. As part of the Source, I am interconnected with everyone, and everything manifested by this Source. Customarily, I call the Source "God," the essence of my being. Compare me to a drop of water from the ocean, carrying the information of the ocean, which has evaporated and will experience being rain before joining and becoming part of the ocean again.

In this current physical lifetime, I arrived in a woman's body in Romania, a district of the earthly homeland. Technically speaking, this body is a spacesuit. All travelers know that to fully experience the visit to Earth, you need the ultimate spacesuit: a body built with local materials using the local life blueprint, also known as the genetic code. The perk of any body is that it carries one of two complementary components, or life seeds, with the information and energy needed for the creation of a new spacesuit for another traveler. These components are masculine and feminine. Bodies are organic and recyclable, so their materials can be used repeatedly for future generations, subjected to time and space. When the two life seeds meet, their life sequences are activated in an explosion of light opening the portal for the spirit that will embody that new creation. It's a miniature big bang, and a new universe is born, the one of a new being. "On earth as it is in heaven."

Let's talk about my arrival or birth, which was no different than any other traveler's. I have known my parents, my sister, and the other significant people in my life as kindred spirits traveling together throughout several previous lives. My body came with a physical *tabula rasa* or blank slate rule running through a program called soul that was created while I was still just a spirit. This birth experience would make me forget my previous lives, meaning that my mind would not retain any conscious memory of them. Why? Because otherwise, it would be impossible to enjoy and fully embrace my current life. Only some of these memories are released by the soul for the benefit of the journey or the spirit's evolution. Once a physical journey is over, the related soul program is archived, and a new one is created, depending upon the next leg of the journey. In spirit, of course, any traveler knows and remembers everything.

Like any soul, my navigation through life uses a mixture of emotions, feelings, thoughts, intuition, and relationships, all guided by spirit, my higher self. The navigation is predestined based upon the information from my previous lives and the current goal of my soul's visit in conjunction with other travelers, all of which has been effortlessly coordinated by Source. Because of that accumulation of pre-existing experiences, I can speak my mother tongue of Romanian, as well as Hungarian, remembered from past lives by simply listening with my heart to the teachings of an extraordinary Hungarian healer, along with English which is my soulmate's language. These languages are subdialects of Human. Human is a dialect of God.

I grew up during a time called communism, which was very dark, both figuratively and literally. One night as a child, I was sitting with my mother outside on the steps of our house. The only light sources were the moon and the stars. As we were talking, I suddenly felt that I was both there and everywhere. I knew everything and had an answer which came directly from Source to any possible question. That spark of enlightenment only lasted for a few seconds, then I returned to being a naïve child, but it was enough to ignite my awakening.

This awakening has also been fueled by my vivid dreams and the information they reveal. They are journeys to worlds where I can fly at any speed, travel through time and interstellar space, interact with parallel universes, materialize things at will, heal sick people, see unseeable things like genetic codes, auras, geopathic radiations, and other phenomena. I visit with those who left the Earth and are now in my spirit family, and also talk to other entities and beings that I label as aliens, angels, Jesus, Heavenly Mother, or God. In my dreams, the solar system was born in the second remembered universe to store the ten principles of the old universe. Under the Sphinx of Romania, there is an ancient library storing the history of mankind. Hungarian is a language passed on from the old universe. Water can be programmed with crystals, sunlight, and prayer to heal ailments. The heart can work like a walkie-talkie and be used to broadcast peace in times of need. Eventually, I started keeping a dream diary, which I hope to share someday.

My life journey in Romania lasted for forty years on a rollercoaster between heaven and hell. The time to end that ride and get a second chance at happiness were both revealed in my dreams. My new destination was Phoenix, Arizona, where I was reborn like the legendary phoenix bird. After living here for more than ten years, I was invited by my "Silver Sisters" to share my thoughts about wisdom. I am still learning and traveling through this life, so sublimating my insight is an ongoing part of this journey, too. Wisdom is the alchemy of transforming knowledge into Love. What would Love say? What would Love do?

Looking back, I see that the catalyst of this alchemy in my present life has been motherhood, the transformation of my body to facilitate the physical arrival of my three amazing children, kindred fellow travelers, together with the expansion of my mindset from "I" to "us," then evolving to "oneness." Love powered the leap of faith to change the course of my life, follow my heart and join my soulmate across the ocean. Love enabled him to gift my children and me the American dream. Love converted coincidence into synchronicity when crossing paths with all the people who have touched my life as I have touched theirs. Sharing this most intimate story about myself with you is also an act of Love.

The more worn my spacesuit, the stronger the Love. It is the bridge across worlds, the element of order, the quintessence of God, my Source. I am a traveler, and this is my personal truth. You also have your personal truth. Thank you for being part of my journey.

Nicoleta Taylor

Nicoleta Taylor was born and lived most of her life in Transylvania, Romania. With a sensitive nature with a passion for reading and writing, she was her high school class valedictorian, also receiving national recognition for her writing skills. This led her to pursue a B.A. in philology, majoring in Romanian and English.

After she became a young mother of three children while living in a small Transylvanian village, she was given a unique work-from-home opportunity with the Ambrosius team, a talented group of wool felt dollmakers. In addition to teaching and dollmaking, enjoying her life in a land rich in myths and legends, she developed a lifelong interest in spirituality. This prompted her to pursue alternative healing arts, with training in Romania, Hungary, and Serbia, ultimately igniting her work as a spiritual healer.

In her forties, she married her American soulmate and moved to Phoenix, Arizona, together with her children, where she rebuilt her life in alignment with the three things she loves doing the most. She has authored courses and teaches Romanian language and culture for several language services providers with outstanding results and feedback from her students. She continues her collaboration with Ambrosius by distributing their exquisitely handcrafted dolls in the U.S. market under the brand name "Eco Flower Fairies." She is now doing the work that makes her soul sing, helping those who seek to complement traditional medicine with a unique holistic spiritual approach, earning her the nickname of "Transylvanian Healer."

nicoleta.taylor@yahoo.com
www.transylvanianhealer.com
www.ecoflowerfairies.com
www.linkedin.com/in/nicoleta-taylor-075a5410

Simply Living
or Living Simply?

By Norma-Jean Strickland

Whenever my friend received a compliment,
he responded with:
"I'm just a mirror!"
"Look in the mirror when you say that!"
"I'm just a reflection of you!"

~ Otto Stein (1904-2004)
Otto Stein Music, Phoenix

Chapter 34

Simply Living or Living Simply?

By Norma-Jean Strickland

Many people at the present time are beginning to live their lives by making more conscious and deliberate decisions. This is a good thing, and I am one of those people. For much of my life, it felt like life was happening *to* me instead of *through* me. There's a huge difference between how that feels and the results you get.

You become wise as you progress through life, no matter your age, once you become your authentic self. This can happen at any time. I'm just in the generation before the concept of authenticity was openly discussed.

After accepting the invitation to be a contributing author for this book, I had to move out of a large house, which I had leased for over six years. The owner wanted to renovate and sell, but generously allowed me six months to find a new place.

This was the very first house I had lived in as an adult, so I made the most of it and FILLED it. I mean, I filled every single inch of it – all the shelves in every cabinet, pantry and closet! All the walls throughout had numerous wall hangings that spoke to me and brought me joy. And THAT doesn't even include the two-car attached garage! It was the first time in over 25 years that I didn't have to pay for external storage. I could actually have ALL my possessions under one roof! There was barely enough room for me to park my SUV. When my father's wife died and he came to live with me briefly, the items in my garage swelled to include some of his material possessions.

Three weeks before our WSS publisher's deadline, I moved from this big house to a small apartment. I went from 1,459 sq. ft. to around 800 sq. ft. Having to downsize in such a major way has been a huge eye-opening experience for me about myself and how I've lived my life. I don't know that I really meant to define myself by the things I owned. I just wanted to be surrounded by beautiful things that I enjoyed and that came to have personal significance.

Moving is never fun and downsizing was easier than I thought it would be. And, of course, doing something like this is always wise, especially since no one is getting any younger! Better to do it now than 10 years from now! It was long overdue.

It didn't take the full six months for me to find a place I loved, so my move was imminent, and downsizing continued in earnest. In that process, I had a bad fall. I was carrying items from the house into the garage, which has a small step. I landed quite hard on both palms and both knees. It took my breath away. I was so stunned that it took a few moments to even get up. Thankfully, no bones were broken. I was just bruised and felt pain.

My neighbors from across the street had come over to help and continued to do so, while I tried to pick myself up off the floor. Even my next-door neighbors started pitching in to help pack. I could not have successfully completed this move without them.

It's so wonderful when you have friends who unexpectedly become a source of emotional encouragement and support. Sometimes their guidance and generosity turn out to be the lifeline thrown to save a drowning soul.

At one point while the movers were busily packing and moving, I just stood in utter disbelief at the amount of material things going by my eyes. It seemed ENDLESS. I burst into tears and asked out loud, *"Am I sick? What is wrong with me?"*

> *"How do you let go of attachments to things? Don't even try. It's impossible. Attachment to things drops away by itself when you no longer seek to find yourself in them."*
>
> ~ Eckhart Tolle, spiritual teacher, and author

Here's a quote that hit me over the head because I realized it described ME:

> *"Clutter is the physical manifestation of unmade decisions fueled by procrastination."*
>
> ~ Anonymous

Well, there it was, and I had to face a hard truth. I had all my possessions under one roof, but I had ignored them. I had taken comfort in knowing that I was surrounded by my "stuff," yet I hadn't taken responsibility for sorting through much of anything. I was living my life, or so I thought. What I had actually done was put my entire life on hold without realizing it.

I am not the same person I was yesterday, last month or last year. As we go through life learning and evolving, it just makes sense to acknowledge when we have outgrown certain things in our lives. This takes courage and involves making deliberate decisions to look deeply at your life – to look deeply IN your life -- to see who you have been, who you are now and who you wish to become.

While engaged in releasing things, I ran across a fabulous quotation:

> *"You can't have everything. Where would you put it?"*
>
> ~ Steven Wright, American stand-up comedian, actor, writer, and Oscar-winning film producer

Getting back to the subject of this book, which is wisdom, the following is one of the acronyms from my first book, "BITE-SIZED PRAYERS: Non-Denominational Morsels to Feed Your Soul," published in late October 2011. It's comprised of 69 one-word concepts or prayers, together with 72 original color photographs I took from various places around the world.

W Waiting

I In

S Silence

D Delivers

O Original

M Messages.

The book was a total surprise. It basically came to me in a dream and was finished in about 72 hours, which included matching all the photographs with specific concepts.

It was one of those experiences you read about when artists, athletes and others talk about being "in the zone." Well, that's what happened for me! I felt like "I" disappeared, and the pen just wrote itself. It was a fascinating experience and one for which I will always be grateful. It's also quite humbling. When Spirit speaks, you need to get out of the way!

Photography and technology have changed dramatically since my book was first published. My goal is to have a second edition with updated photographs and new concepts.

Long story short (HA!!), I have come to believe very strongly in the body-mind-spirit holistic approach to life. It just makes sense. There's a wonderful book by Louise Hay entitled, "You Can Heal Your Life," published in 1984. She includes a list of physical problems with their probable cause. I'm still recovering from the fall I took and my left hip has caused nearly constant pain with great difficulty in walking. This doesn't seem like ME!

In her book, Louise lists the following probable cause for hip problems:

"Fear of going forward in major decisions. Nothing to move forward to."

Again, this hit me like a ton of bricks.

My commitment is to live intentionally.

"Gratitude turns what we have into enough."

~ Aesop,
Greek storyteller (620 – 564 BCE)

My heart is filled with gratitude! I am enough and I have enough!

Norma-Jean Strickland

My life is a wonderful unfolding of creative expression! I'm a writer, educator, speaker, classical musician, photographer, colorful character and curious creature! I have had the privilege of touching the lives of thousands of people in meaningful ways. My vision is to delight and bring joy, love and healing to the human heart through music, story and play! I am seeking opportunities to collaborate and look forward to hearing from you!

WEBSITES:
https://njstrickland.wixsite.com/starlightcreativepro
https://www.linkedin.com/in/normajeanstrickland/

Scan Me!

I Brought It with Me

By Pam Schuler

*"You've got to go out on a limb sometimes
because that's where the fruit is."*

~ Will Rogers

Chapter 35

I Brought It with Me

By Pam Schuler

I have literally traveled the world. It did not seem that would be my path early in my life, growing up on a farm in rural America. The concept of travel was extremely limited, but when I boarded my first airplane at 19 for a three-month backpacking trip through Europe, I realized that a vastly different future was available for me, and it had come to me with a whimsical decision.

Almost every big decision or move in my life has been made by intuition speaking loudly to small suggestions. I may have felt isolated growing up but with this first big bold move, I realized a sense of control and direction in my life.

My early years were spent living miles from the nearest neighbors and even further from friends. Extended family was about 90 miles away, so my brother and I created our own entertainment and mystery worlds. My best friends were creatures of fur and nature, including a special tree that was both friend and counselor. That tree was the best listener but also offered a lot of wisdom.

In retrospect, I wish I had discovered my skills as a photographer earlier and captured even more of my observations on paper. I had a natural ability to write, but in a failed attempt to support my story-telling, my mother required writing which drove the interest under-ground. I have known that I was a storyteller for a long time but have struggled to embrace it, only more recently letting the world experi-ence my stories in word and visual formats.

During the year of the Covid lockdown, I caught myself finding comfort and purpose in revisiting and sharing myself as I reconnected with journals and photos of many years of exploring.

Throughout the years, I have heard the judgment of others that "those who spend major time behind a camera are not experiencing the moment." I hold this to be a big lie, at least in my case. Being behind a camera allows me to focus on an event or location, much like I deal with most of my life. I first take in the big picture to capture the overall impression, and then I look for the close-up or details that make the situation tick. I capture it all. The best part of this personal approach is that I get to really connect in the present and, with great ease, reconnect later through words and photos.

The energy of the actual experience is immediately registered as I permit myself to fully be present, and later, I can travel energetically to those places or people at any time.

Some people are surprised when someone they have been thinking about is suddenly at the other end of a phone call or at their door. I regard this as totally normal, knowing that we are energetically con-nected and just decide to make physical contact.

Throughout my working years, I learned to capture connections daily in face-to-face interactions. I was blessed with having access to a wide variety of people who often appeared in my space needing guidance or clarity. I came to understand that I was paid to do the job that I willingly performed but that my real work was these more mys-tical connections. Like most people who discover their hidden gifts, I was at times reluctant to offer what I was being told to share. But I developed a check-in process with that strange feeling that would appear near my left side. When a message appears for me, I always ask, "Is this meant to be shared?" When I receive the affirmation, I know that most of the words that will be flowing from me will not be mine and are meant for the higher good.

Some refer to this kind of message sharing as psychic or channeling. I just think of it as normal. These daily interactions proved to be as memorable as those I created while traveling.

Leaving my full-time employment for retirement was filled with anxiety and apprehension. I was concerned that my personal connections would no longer exist. Was I leaving not only the source of income but also my greater work? Would I be able to travel even more? I had checked off many of the major trips but there were a few more.

For the first few years of retirement, I found it surprisingly easy to find people who were still being led to me. I drove for Lyft and had amazing connections even through short rides with about 70% of them being channeled a message. I stepped up my wedding officiant business and was blessed with many amazing experiences and even allow Mrs. Claus to take up residency in my home each December with a full schedule of her own. Post-retirement trips to Cambodia, Thailand, Turkey, and Egypt were added to my list and still saw me with my now blond-white hair and backpack setting off to make more connections.

Covid shut down almost all these alternative connections as it did for everyone around the world. A familiar visitor, depression, tried to establish residency and bleak days seemed the norm.

In August, nature conspired to rescue me as two beautiful black kittens were planted in a large flowerpot on my back patio by a feral mom. Despite her hissing protests and the constant moving of the babies, I spoiled them and was determined that they could someday become well-behaved house cats. I really did not know day to day how long I would be permitted to be a part of their lives, but I documented their growth and kitten antics in word and photos/videos. The Kitten Chronicles came to be a regular post of my Facebook personality. The little boy, Sam Patrick, is currently lounging on the cat tree at nearly nine pounds.

Over time, the little girl and several other members of my feral backyard gang sadly moved on. Most recently, my dedicated 17-year-old feline friend, the Mystical, Magical, Marvelous Madison, also passed. All things change, but thankfully, I have so many memories of them all, connections recorded in words and images I captured along the way.

The connections that were made early in life and my many heart-to-heart adventures came forward to comfort me in this forced isolation over 60. All those experiences have been stored in a metaphoric backpack that I have worn since my first big adventure. They live with me. I will never stop traveling or capturing my experiences if I have the choice. In my darkest times, those words and photos have always proved to be my true friends.

Pam Schuler

I'm a compassionate, Re-Passioned, world traveler, humanity lover, pet Mom, and much more.

I was raised, studied, and taught high school in rural Nebraska. Phoenix, Arizona, has been my home for nearly forty years.

Shocking my parents, I took off a semester from college; I backpacked through Europe with a friend and began a life-long interest in a plethora of cultures, archeological sites, and discovering myself. My journey has included worldwide travel, studies of most major religions, humanitarian volunteerism, working directly with college students, and mentoring others as I continue to learn and grow.

When I retired after 25 years at the local community colleges, I feared that my direct access to opportunities to serve was gone. Instead, I am re-passioned and finding new ways to be of service to a higher calling. Currently, I officiate weddings and hand-fasting's, serve as a Pet Nana to all kinds of creatures (I "Sit and Stay"), and allow Mrs. Claus to visit and play in December.

Website: www.ritesofcelebration.com
Facebook: https://www.facebook.com/ritesofcelebration
Instagram: https://www.instagram.com/ritesofcelebration/

Sea Glass

By Patricia Holgate Haney

*"You cannot always control what goes on outside.
But you can always control what goes on inside."*
*"Everything you need you already have. You are a whole,
total person, not an apprentice person on the way to
someplace else."*

~ Wayne Dyer

Chapter 36

Sea Glass

By Patricia Holgate Haney

From a young age, I was always curious, a seeker. Dad was an avid reader; our bookshelves overflowed with every genre, and I read them all. My fascination with travel was fueled by immersing myself in books where I visited exotic places and participated in witty conversations. My Grandparents and Great Aunt further inspired me with their trips to India, China, the Middle East, and other faraway destinations. They detailed their travels in eloquent hand-written letters, which I waited anxiously for Ralph, our postman, to deliver. I watched their slides, photos, and sometimes movies when they returned.

From the time I can remember, I was the first one in the car. When my grandparents took me along on road trips, I was beside myself with joy. Oh, the glory of unfolding a map or road atlas following the roads. The destination didn't matter; I just wanted to go! While friends dreamed of horses and dolls, I dreamed of having a car and traveling anywhere I wanted.

I grew up in a multi-cultural rural area surrounded by orange groves and dairy farms. Hard-working families were chasing the dream. I was curious about their customs, their family histories, and religions. I was described as "a little old girl" because I loved to sit in the kitchen with the adults, watch them cook, learn about their backgrounds, take part in their customs, and explore their faith. I always wanted to know more.

During my exploration of faith, there were many different experiences in the religious services. Some were loud and joyful, others sedate and quiet. They all were fascinating, but fascination turned to fear during one service when the minister yelled that we were all sinners and going to hell if we didn't repent. Around me, people began speaking in tongues; I didn't understand what was happening. I just knew I was sorry for whatever I had done and didn't want to be yelled at or go to hell. Those devils dancing among the flames scared the crap out of me, and I never went back.

I worried about dying. Would I be in a mystical, magical place where angels played trumpets, happy and beautiful in flowing robes amongst the clouds, or was I going straight to the depths of hell? Or, heaven help me, would I remain in limbo? Would I belong anywhere? The more I explored religion, the more questions I had. Not good enough, bad enough, or not enough period. Pieces of my soul vanished as I doubted my worthiness.

A column in our newspaper featured tales of local people and places. When I was ten, I wrote to the columnist and enclosed a story. He invited me to the newsroom. The air was thick with cigarette smoke, reporters furiously typing; then, in front of me was the man in the photo from our paper. Kind, he encouraged me to continue writing. I remember how I felt more than what he said. I had been searching for validation; this was a start.

Attending college was intoxicating. A wide variety of subjects opened even more doors to explore. I fell in love during college, but after a few years and two children, our marriage imploded, and we divorced. My children are blessings in my life, and I was fortunate to receive an additional gift that I will always treasure, his Mom, Gloria, who became a lifelong friend and travel buddy. We have a similar passion for reading, travel, exploration, and laughter. We made memories on many road trips and explored Europe together. Close friends and some family shunned me because I had divorced, so it was even sweeter to have Gloria in my life.

Your Erroneous Zones by Wayne Dyer had just been published and was on the curriculum when I returned to college. His book became a catalyst in my journey of self-discovery.

"Everything you need you already have.
You are a whole, total person, not an apprentice person
on the way to someplace else."

~ Wayne Dyer.

Ever curious, I continued taking courses throughout life. I kept reading, attending workshops, and searching for what I thought was missing. I began to change my mindset.

"Knowledge has entertained me, and it has shaped me,
and it has failed me.
Something in me still starves"

~ Mary Oliver.

While attending a workshop, I learned to look inward, finally understanding that my self-worth was based solely on my perception, and I realized I had been selling myself short.

The first thing I changed was to start each day with gratitude. I reminded myself daily to be mindful and began to journal.

I reflected on examples of strong women in my life who gave their time and resources to help others. They did so with a sense of gratitude and kindness. Following their lead, I realized I had something to offer. I could give time, listen, and reach out. In return, I began to feel my heart open.

Eventually, I discovered life did not have a map; it was an unexpected journey of ups, downs, and potholes. A glorious ride, my journey was better than I had ever imagined. Harboring hurt, anger, and self-doubt, I had missed beauty along the way. Practicing gratitude changed my outlook and life.

I began to forgive others for hurting me; more importantly, to forgive myself. I didn't forget but decided not to allow the negative to overshadow the good. I learned that our natural state is that of oneness and began to practice self-acceptance. Living in the past had prevented me from experiencing life in the present.

On vacation, I saw sea glass for the first time; I was intrigued and determined to learn more about it. Broken and discarded pieces of glass and china tumble in the seas for years, randomly landing on a beach. Sea glass over time becomes polished with smooth edges and frosted. A miraculous occurrence just as we are. It clicked.

Curiosity and willingness to try new things had enabled me to experience unique places and people and brought me joy. I no longer searched for missing pieces; I began to appreciate all my experiences as part of the journey.

Walking the beach, I saw glittering speckles of color in the sand. I thought of all the pieces of myself I had searched for throughout life. I realized sea glass was a lot like me. Time had smoothed out some of my rough edges, and sea glass became a symbol for my journey. I was not broken or missing any pieces; I was gaining value. My life is a precious miracle—a gift that keeps evolving.

We may make mistakes or question the journey but remember this; when we begin life, we are a vessel in which we store our life experiences. Our vessel continually fills; it does not break. We must learn from our life events; resolve to live so that someday we don't need to wish to tell our younger self anything.

I am God's jewel becoming perfect imperfection. I am attempting to live life to the fullest; I navigate my journey. The journey is my prize, and I cherish every moment of it.

Patricia Holgate Haney

Patricia Holgate Haney has had a passion for travel since she jumped in the backseat of the family car on trips to "anywhere and nowhere." The fascination expanded with the exotic international travel her Grandparents and Great Aunt shared through photos and airmailed letters. Travel became a goal inspired by her love of books passed down by her father. She immersed herself in the written word and became lost in the world she experienced. She has always been a searcher, both in the spiritual sense and in travel. Grateful for her journey to date, she continues to study and practice mindfulness, gratitude, kindness and is dedicated to becoming a positive light for others.

A travel professional, ordained minister, paralegal, and after careers in both the for-profit and nonprofit world, her passions for travel as well as writing continue

She has been published in two compilation books; *Love Meets Life* and *Ordinary Oneness*.

She and her husband Gary enjoy travel, cooking, and spending time with their family, including two sons, Kevin and Josh Catalfo, three grandchildren, and three great-grandchildren. She volunteers for organizations that are dedicated to helping the underserved and ensuring equality for all

You can reach her by e-mail at seaglass@phtravels.com,
Website: https://phtravels.com/
Twitter and Instagram: phtravels

Scan Me!

The Power of Sophia Transforms Us for Justice

By Rev. PJ Boone-Edgerton Longoni

"For wisdom…is a reflection of eternal light, a spotless mirror of the working of God, and an image of his goodness…she passes into holy souls and makes them friends of God, and prophets."

~ (Wisdom 7:26-27)

Chapter 37

The Power of Sophia Transforms us for Justice

Rev. PJ Boone-Edgerton Longoni

Recently, I facilitated a workshop exploring human values (truth, right action, love, peace, non-violence) and the concept, justice. I was compelled to do the workshop because of the death of George Floyd in 2020. It broke my heart when he called out to his mother. Symbolically, I see it as him calling out to the Divine Feminine for mercy and justice. His cry was a call to be delivered from the masculine militarized energy acting out in this terrible situation. I was pushed to do the workshop because of my belief that to bring about justice in this world and to improve our social relationships, we have to do interior work on ourselves – just as so many of our prominent human rights leaders have done for decades – and to pick up their mantle.

As a visual person, the easiest place for me to begin my research on the meaning of justice was to explore our prominent image of Lady Justice, a silent and demure figure who has graced the doors of our legal institutions for many years. This contemporary symbol of justice shows her blindfolded, carrying a scale and a sword – reminding those entering courthouses that the administration of justice should be objective, swift and free from corruption.

The blindfold over Lady Justice's eyes demonstrates that she is not influenced by outside forces. The balanced scale she holds suggests that – once the court reaches an objective state – it fairly examines the facts. The sword that Lady Justice holds "symbolizes enforcement and respect and means that justice stands by its decision and ruling, and is able to take action." What is not discussed about any of these symbols is her power, her "mother love," which protects, defends, and balances our hearts and minds so that justice can be served.

Some images of Lady Justice show her not only holding a scale, but also with an ancient symbol of two entwined serpents. These represent the Kundalini which, in Eastern traditions, is the essential energy, more fundamental than nuclear power, that is the basis of who we are and all that we experience. It is believed that Kundalini energy awakens and evolves certain areas of the spine known as the chakras. As these energy centers awaken and become more aligned and balanced, an individual's consciousness changes. Essentially, how s/he perceives and responds to the world changes.

I am the Executive Director of The Tadini House. I work with families whose loved ones are facing a criminal case. I have found that justice is made elusive by the rules of the criminal court system and that there is an imbalance in our judicial system. The imbalance leads society more towards punishment rather than towards rehabilitation and restoration. This imbalance has imprisoned many fathers and mothers for forgivable offenses, whose children have ended up in foster care as a result.

The Sentencing Project is a Washington, D.C.-based research and advocacy center working for decarceration or to reduce the use of incarceration in the United States and to address racial disparities in the criminal justice system. Their research shows that the United States is the world's leader in incarceration with two million people currently in the nation's prisons and jails – a 500% increase over the last forty years. The harshness of our laws has been cited as a key issue leading to these statistics.

A call for an interior balance is not only represented by Lady Justice today but arises from an ancient and powerful symbol – Ma'at, an Egyptian Goddess. Ma'at was the goddess of truth, justice, balance, and, most importantly, order. However, Ma'at was more than just a goddess to the ancient Egyptians. She represented the crucial concept of how the universe was maintained. The ancient Egyptians believed that the universe had an order to it, and it was Ma'at who kept everything in balance. This helped the ancient Egyptians develop a strong sense of morality and justice. Ma'at was extremely important in attaining the Afterlife. According to Ancient Egyptian mythology, after the death of the body, everyone had to pass through the Hall of Judgment, where a person's heart was weighed on a scale against Ma'at's feather of truth. If the deceased person's heart balanced with Ma'at's feather, they could continue their journey to the Afterlife. If not, their journey ended. This influenced the daily actions of the ancient Egyptians.

In our modern western society, how do we balance our hearts and minds in order to bring about the justice represented by Ma'at?

In preparing for the workshop, I also researched various esoteric teachings. I found another powerful feminine figure – Sophia, Goddess of Wisdom. Sophia essentially embodies the knowledge of spiritual mysteries. An image of Sophia is not at all like that of Lady Justice. Instead, Sophia is portrayed with her eyes wide open, not blindfolded, with a scale that represents inner balance. Sophia has sometimes been portrayed as a cosmic ordering principle, as universal architect, and as mediator of all scientific knowledge. Sophia defines experiences as having spiritual or philosophical meaning, which can inspire awe, beauty, dignity and grace.

Wisdom teachings from around the world help us to balance our energy and bring us to the fullest capacity to act from love in order to serve humankind. I strongly believe that wisdom instructs, defends, guides, and leads us toward justice and so much more!

Now, when I think of George Floyd's death, I will no longer think of Lady Justice standing silent and blindfolded with her sword turned down. I will see the warrior Sophia, standing with her sword over her head, cutting what is holding us back and giving her clarion call for justice.

Lady Justice, Sophia, Ma'at, Kundalini energy, the chakras, balancing our bodies and emotions – all these images strengthen my belief that if we want to see justice in our world, we each have to do the interior work necessary to create justice and fairness in our own lives.

Rev. P J Boone-Edgerton Longoni

As a mother of two men impacted by the criminal justice system, Rev. PJ Boone-Edgerton Longoni understands the importance of providing beautiful, safe spaces and time for returning citizens to help them ease back into society.

She founded the Tadini House (TH) to make a difference for men like her two sons. Rev. PJ first began her ministry by offering her participants guidance and opportunities for personal growth. She also pointed participants toward needed services. Today, Rev. PJ offers religious services at The Shrine of Holy Wisdom, Tempe, AZ, and at TH's Chapel of the Sacred Heart. She is building a community of people interested in serving the formerly incarcerated. Rev. PJ provides healing services and workshops for TH participants in conjunction with sister organizations, Aspiring Onward and The Creative Flame.

Website: www.thetadinihouse.org

Scan Me!

Wise at Sixteen

By Sandy Rogers

"Turn your wounds into wisdom."

~ Oprah Winfrey

Chapter 38

Wise at Sixteen

By Sandy Rogers

You might say a 16-year-old girl could not be wise. Or that she hasn't had enough life experience to possess the wisdom to make adult decisions.

One definition of wisdom is:

"**Wisdom**. . .is the ability to think and act using knowledge, experience, understanding, common sense, and insight."

Here's a definition of wise:

"**Wise**. . .mean(s) having or showing sound judgment. **Wise** suggests a great understanding of people and situations."

By these definitions, yes, a 16-year-old could be wise and possess the wisdom to make adult decisions.

It was 1963, and I had just turned 15 in June. The new school year was in full swing in the small town in Ohio, where I lived with my mother, father, and three younger siblings. I had been attending this school since kindergarten.

I was a sophomore in high school with a class of fewer than 100 students. The popular girls were smart or cheerleaders, or on the drill team, or were the pretty girls. I wasn't one of them. I was barely five feet tall, with unruly brown hair, and was painfully shy. When I was three years old, I started dance classes, which was my creative outlet. When the opportunity came to try out for the drill team, I took it. When I got chosen, it put me in the "in-crowd!" Performing on the drill team made me feel special. Like I mattered. And my shyness disappeared.

That fall, a new boy enrolled in school. He never shared why his family moved to our town from Kentucky. He was good-looking, tall, with curly blond hair and blue eyes. He quickly became part of the in-crowd and the object of attention with the popular girls.

The fall dance was in October, and I had never had a date. When the new boy asked if I wanted to go to the dance, I was beyond surprised! He was a year older and already driving. To my amazement, when I asked my parents if I could go, they said, "Yes." On the Saturday night of the dance, he picked me up. Naturally, he had to come to the door, so my parents could "give their approval."

My stomach was churning with excitement as we entered the gymnasium decorated in brilliant fall colors. The popular girls were visibly shocked when they saw us walk in together. We had a wonderful evening, and I was on cloud nine.

He drove me home and, to my disbelief, wanted to kiss me. That kiss led to more kissing, which led to making out, which led to "doing it." I didn't know I was doing anything wrong! Yes, first date, first kiss, and first time doing it! Looking back, I realize my mother never gave me "the talk." You know, the one about sex and how you get pregnant.

Six weeks passed, and we had a few more dates. It was the Sunday after Christmas, and my mother asked if I let him touch me. I wondered what she meant, which she then explained in detail. She realized that I hadn't had my period. My mother became enraged! "How could you do that?" she screamed.

The next thing I knew, she called our family doctor. He told her to bring me to his office, where he would examine me. I had never had "that" exam before and didn't know what was happening. I was scared. After the exam, he told her I was about six weeks pregnant. I don't remember a lot of what happened after that. I do remember my mother was furious at me.

When we got home, she and my father sat me down and decided that the boy and I had to get married because they didn't want an illegitimate grandchild. Their anger was frightening.

Everyone went back to school on the Monday after Christmas break. On Tuesday, my parents, the boy's parents, and he and I went to the county courthouse. The ceremony was performed and ensured this baby would be "legitimate."

I went to school the next day and was called into the principal's office. He asked two questions: "Are you pregnant?" and "Did you get married yesterday?" Of course, I answered honestly. He said I had to leave school immediately. Remember, this was January 1964. Things were very different back then. By the way, the boy didn't have to leave school. I never saw him again after that day at the courthouse when we "got married."

Ironically, my parents put me in a home for unwed mothers, but I was legally married! This "home" was like a prison. It was an old, three-story mansion. The first floor had the offices, kitchen and dining room. The second floor was the labor and delivery room, nursery, and solarium for the girls to use during their free time. Next to that was a wooden phone booth with a door that closed to provide privacy. We could only use the phone for a few hours a day. The rest of the time, it was chained and padlocked. The third floor was the dormitory with a community bath and shower for the ten girls who were residents.

One of the many rules was that we couldn't use our real names. I have blocked out so many memories of that time that I don't remember what name I chose. The reasoning for the name change was so our "secret" would be safe. The secret that we were unwed mothers and family and friends wouldn't know we were pregnant. They just knew we "went away to Aunt Mary's for the summer."

When I was going into my ninth month of pregnancy, my mother informed me that if I came home and kept this baby after giving birth, it would be raised as my brother or sister – not as my child! Some part of me couldn't imagine doing that.

I turned 16 in June and gave birth on August 2 in that God-forsaken place. I pleaded with the nurse not to show me the baby or reveal the gender. I couldn't bear to know anything for fear of not being able to part with my baby and then being forced to pretend to be his or her sister instead of mother.

A few days later, my mother took me home. She forbade me to ever discuss this. Over the years, I wanted to, but she always refused. I learned that she not only knew the gender of my child but had also seen the baby. During the Christmas holidays, eleven years later, she finally told me that I had had a son.

You can imagine that there is much more to this story. Twenty years after my son was born, we were reunited on his 20th birthday, when we spoke for the first time.

Was it wise to give up my son, who would be my only child? The pain of loss and grieving are still with me, even though our reunion was thirty-eight years ago. I regret my decision, but deep in my soul, I know it was the best one for my son and me.

Wisdom comes in complex ways. And, yes, a 16-year-old can make a wise decision.

Sandy Rogers

Sandy Rogers has been doing business in the Metropolitan Phoenix, Arizona market since 1992. Her peers know her as "The Referral Queen." Sandy has been serving entrepreneurs in the holistic health, metaphysical, spiritual, and personal development conscious business communities since 2000 through email promotions, Marketing 101 consulting, event production, eAnnouncements, and networking.

Known for her engaging smile and warm heart, Sandy's vast experience includes 40 plus years of expertise in corporate sales, marketing and administration with creative entrepreneurial networking skills to build her list of connections and to assist others with their business needs.

In 2005, she received certification from the Referral Institute® as a Certified Networker® Professional ("CNP"). Sandy's mission is to be the resource and connector for those who want to grow their small business through the power of referrals, through building relationships and through word-of-mouth marketing.

In addition to being a Master Networker and living her passion, Sandy is the founder of several entrepreneurial businesses providing a variety of resources for entrepreneurs, solopreneurs authors, inventors, speakers, healthcare and wellness professionals.

Sandy is a published author of "The 5 Year Journal" and "Love Meets Life". She is a birthmother who surrendered her only child to adoption in 1964. She is an advocate for adoption reform and, in 1985, helped create new law in Kentucky that allowed adult adoptees to petition the courts for their original birth certificates. In 2020, she testified in the Arizona Legislature for similar law changes.

Contact information:
Sandy@AskSandyRogers.com
http://www.asksandyrogers.com
https://5yearjournal.com
https://www.facebook.com/Sandy4Help
https://www.linkedin.com/in/sandyrogersreferrals

Scan Me!

The Way of the Writerly

By Sharyn G. Jordan

"I had learned already never to empty the well of my writing but always to stop when there was still something there in the deep part of the well, and let it refill at night from the springs that fed it."

~ Ernest Hemingway

Chapter 39

The Way of the Writerly

By Sharyn G. Jordan

The Writerly Journey is as sacred, magical and/or pragmatic as we, the storyteller, desire. Scribes of mythic tales, seers of the mighty winds sweeping positive change across the land and luminous visionaries, we are creating a new future, now. If ever there was a time when we Writerlies were in demand, it is now. Let us align ourselves in the timeless states of grace, where exquisite epiphanies dwell. Based on how we have honed our talents, our adaptability and deepened our capacity for unconditional love, we are sojourners walking through this divine life, able to make it up as we go. We are time travelers calling forth our ancient muses, creating noble, influential narratives that elegantly reshape our tomorrows in ways of transformational worthiness, dignity, and glorious compassion. Throughout our ongoing life-after-life, we have worked through many cycles, phases, and ages, and, yes, stages that brought us here. Indeed, no more waiting. We have arrived!

Vividly, I recall the first time when I stepped into the sacred art of story. At the age of four, on our annual summer trek to the enchanted forest of Ruidoso, New Mexico, I found myself listening to the evergreen trees whisper their wisdom, breathing in the earth's musky fragrances, and being enthralled with every bird's song. 'Twas the year my parents began a custom of taking my younger sister, sweet Suzanne, and me to the neighboring Cloudcroft tribal area for cultural awareness, to delight in their sacred dances, and to hand-select our souvenirs. The curio shoppe was filled with an array of feathered headdresses, shelves full of mystical crystals, colorful dresses adorned with countless rows of rickrack, beautifully crafted moccasins, and dream catchers. It was fantastical. I can still smell the cypress wafting through the air. Sitting upon a cobalt-blue velvet cloth was a gorgeous cedar treasure box, a little brass lock in the shape of a heart with its very own key. Upon opening it, my heart began to race as though it would leap out of my little chest! Inside was a soft, sable brown, leather-bound book engraved with the golden words of *"Dearest Diary."*

Mother asked the storekeeper if *"Dearest"* was perhaps a translation error or even a misprint. In impeccable English, he politely, rather mystically, replied, "Since writing is sacred, the person who carved the cedar chest sewed the parchment pages into the diary and intentionally engraved the words *"Dearest"* was one and the same. He honors that we are here as Soul Story Scribes." Thankfully, my dad overheard this interesting exchange, and took the liberty to write it as my first *"Dearest Diary"* entry. At the time, I could read and write simple words, yet, deep down, I trusted I would grow into its bright promises.

Returning to our cabin in the woods, I was enamored with the book's back section. It was brimming with sketches of forest animals, butterflies, and birds, complete with written symbolism. Included was a decoded chart of a memory system for shamans, diviners, and medicine men. At that time, this information was way over my head. However, as dad read us the pages of tribal lore, dream language, and cultural heroes, they sounded like the nightly fairy tales he read to Suzanne and me.

In retrospect, I'm certain that answering the call of this lifetime's Writerly mission was first clarified by dad reading Suzanne and me bedtime stories. Well-versed in the joys of experiential enrichments, his brilliant influence continues to inspire my path. I, too, have chosen to help others scribe their legacy, bring Heaven to Earth, and, to evolve. His passion for story deepened my creative resources, expanded my imagination, and up leveled my innate innovative abilities. Through the archetypal fairy tale characters, I learned how challenges – and their eventual overcoming – were always an opportunity to boldly rise above.

Our nightly adventures consisted of Brothers Grimm *Fairy Tales*, Robert Louis Stevenson's *Treasure Island,* Lewis Carrol's *Alice in Wonderland,* JRR Tolkien's *Lord of the Rings* trilogy, and of course, C. S. Lewis' seven-book *Narnia* series. In addition, Rudyard Kipling's *Jungle Book*, our favorite Bible stories, and – oh, yes, since dad was a friend of fellow Rotarian, Norman Vincent Peale – Guidepost's inspirational stories was in our regular reading rotation. Gladly, we practiced Dr. Peale's positivity! Upon completing our amazing story-time every night, dad sang *Row, Row, Your Boat*, encouraging Suzanne and me to "Discover the Wisdom hidden within each experience. Just like our stories, anything and everything is possible. So, dream, write, and create a happily-ever-after life. Joy is a choice."

I knew how blessed I was to have him as my dad. Generously, he served Humanity's greater good, was devoted to BEing the Difference, and was also a gifted storyteller. I continued to steep myself in legends, folklore, and history. By the time I was eight years young, these age-old teachings, their mystical messages, and journaling became part of my everyday life. Sadly, right before my thirteenth birthday, my dear father became gravely ill. For the next five months, he lived in the hospital, only coming home for Christmas and Valentine's Day. With my mother right by his side, our grandmother moved in with us. Thankfully, I visited dad every afternoon. Reading aloud his favorite Zane Gray hardback novels, Erle Stanley Gardner, Perry

Mason's courtroom dramas, and beloved fairy tales he so enthusiastically shared with us. "Twas full circle.

My dad was still hospitalized when, on the morning of April 7th, I was awakened at 2:22 a.m., hearing his distinctive voice. I immediately sat up only to realize I was alone. It was dad speaking to me in my heart, saying, "I am leaving now, yet I will always be with you. Keep Writing." The phone rang. I heard Grandmother crying; it was the hospital calling to say, my hero, dad had died at only age thirty-eight. These unforgettable experiences persist to inform my decisions in ways I continue to see as synchronistic. After my dad transitioned, I developed an even keener passion for writing articles, short stories, poems, personal letters, and biographies for family members who have also passed over. Navigating the uncertain waters of life as a teenager without a dad, I left home at sixteen, determined to map my own destiny The HeART of Scribing is my Safe Haven. The process of writing my joys, sorrows, accomplishments, perceptions, fears, and tears will forever be a gift, revealing a much deeper understanding of life itself. In honor of my dad, as Soul Story Scribes, we Rise Above.

"Do not worry. You have always written before; you will write now."

~ Ernest Hemingway

Writerlies, Wordsmithers

Wisdom-Keepers, Authors

Magical Memoirists, Muses

Dream-Weavers, Anthologists

Legacy Creators, Myth-Makers

Soul Sojourners, Time Travelers

Scripters, Archivists, Biographers

Dear Diarists, Joy-filled Journalers

Poets, Prosers, Psalmists, Novelists

Fantasiers, Faerie Talers, Folklorers

Sacred Scribers, Sublime Storytellers

Divine Alchemists, Treasure Mappers

Mystery Suspensers, Spiritual Penners

Journalists, Dissertationlists, Editorialists

Business Theorists, Coach Motivationists

Short Storiers, Detectives, Western Genres

Thriller Spinners, Spy Crafters, Ink Slingers

Historical Fictioners, Romancing the Stoners

Self-Helpers, Symbolizers, Crime Gumshoers

Sci-Fiers, YA Adventurers, Politico Comediers

Children Literary-er, Magnificent Opus Oraclers

Celestial Ode-ers, Sonnet Celebrators, Lexiconers

Content Cultivators, Instagrammers, #Hashtaggers

Sharyn Jordan

Sharyn has merged the practical with the magical, spiritual and scientific. As an agent of positive change, she continuously refines, defines and aligns Soul's inner sanctum and Home's alchemy. She is a published author of eight books, The Home Whisperer, Environmental Healer, founder of the Feng Shui Simplified Consulting Firm, established in 1994; has an online Wind-Water-Writerly series entitled the BEjeweled Treasure Mapping process, which teaches how to call forth the muse.

Learning these sacred principles in 1975 when Sharyn owned Rosebud Preschool, she was keenly aware that her precious three sons, then ages four, three, and one, would be in high school at the same time. Oh, yes, teenaged boys have hollow legs!

With the unique Mapping now known as Vision Boarding, still eons ahead of its time, she intended to have a family business. Indeed, that very year was 1989, which found Sharyn and her BEloved husband, Jay, opening a movie theater, and growing it into a multi-million-dollar enterprise. Honored to serve their Arizona White Mountain community for twelve years, they wisely sold it due to Jay's failing health. This fulfilled another dream-come-true of traveling extensively for the next eleven magical years. After forty-two amazing years of marriage, her darling Jay peacefully transitioned in February 2012. Sharyn is BEyond Grateful to BE a loving Gramma of fourteen GRANDchildren, answering to each of her three special names: Gawni, Baby Poppa or NiNi. She adores bringing Heaven to Earth, CUPPA Calls, creating poetry from her HeART, reading and writing.

Website (currently being redesigned): https://fengshuisimplified.com/
Email: Greetings@SharynGJordan.Agency
https://www.facebook.com/TheHomeWhispererFengShuiSimplified/
https://www.instagram.com/sharynjordan/

Scan Me!

Cougar Mountain

By Shenayda Linda Deane

"Reality is now. It is always in motion, always dynamic, never static, always changing. Only the story we tell ourselves about reality is static. The concepts we entertain about a past or a future, contribute to our missing out on experiencing reality in the present."

~ Dr. Robert Gibson (a teacher of teachers)

Chapter 40

Cougar Mountain

By Shenayda Linda Deane

It was the Oregon mountains calling to me, so green and lush. I could feel moisture filling my nostrils when I arrived. This was the first day of my vision quest. We ate and drank, knowing the next day we were headed for the mountain, and we would not be eating or drinking for the next four days.

The first wisdom teaching and practice was preparing prayer ties, which consisted of a 2-inch square of red material. We began praying in silence for hours at a time as we placed tobacco and sage in each tie, praying for our own healing and for all our relations, including mother earth and all planetary bodies. The energy was strong and powerful as we filled our pouches. I realized we were sending blessings, and as we tied each pouch, it activated the universal law of sending and receiving. I began to realize that this whole journey, now, as well as life itself, was about releasing until that time when we finally relinquish our bodies. In the morning, the ties would go into the fire on the mountain to be released.

We were to do two sweats, one before and one after we returned from the four days on the mountain. There were four dedicated people who prepared the home camp on the mountain. Their job was to pray for us, keep the fire going for the time we were out in the forest and also to eat for us.

The evening of the first day was time to do what is called a Native sweat which was guided by the local native leaders. Sunset brought us to our first Native American sweat for the quest. The best way to explain this is by using the Native Americana words: purification, thanking Great Spirit for our ancestors, and surrender. The prayers and songs take place in four rounds, each bringing us to forgiveness and to return to the womb and back.

In order to describe the lodge, there is a combination of the tree people and the stone people. Hides, blankets and mother earth make up the components along with a lot of prayer. The complete balance of fire, earth, air and water combines to make a womb of surrender. To truly understand this, it has to be experienced.

The first day:
To Cougar Mountain we go. I am taken back to ten years prior when my first Native American teacher, Sun Bear, took us on an underworld journey to discover our power animal at our birth. Mine was a mother cougar. I asked myself as the cougar came to me in the mountains of Arizona, what does she mean to me and my nature? The answer came, she was protective, courageous and devoted to her cubs. She was not a human predator, but if threatened, she would fight, not run. She was my guide on this quest.

As it was time to leave, I quietly started up the mountain to find my sitting place. The higher I got, the more my instincts kicked in and I saw a giant Hemlock tree that had fallen seasons ago. The rain and snow had worn out a bed of thin shavings that fit my 5-foot 8-inch body. This was to be my place, leaving only to relieve myself over the next four days. On top of the tree, I placed my blanket and pipe. I was to smoke my pipe as needed for strength and courage.

I drifted in and out of the life I had lived up until that time, beginning as early as I could remember, trusting where it would take me.

It became clear when unresolved or confusing times came to my memories. I was then taken into sleep or dream time each day and was visited by animals feeding and the wonder of their beauty. The days and nights folded into each other, and my mind became clearer and more sensitive to what came forth from my experiences. The details regarding events began to unfold. I now saw what happened at the time and knew what truths lay hidden under the actual events. It was like watching a movie, as my emotions released true insights from my body through tears, anger and loss. I realized I could only do and feel what I was capable of at the time and the clarity was washing me clean.

I reevaluated decisions I had made which shifted my choices in life. One such event was most profound. I was in my twenties and was at a vulnerable changing point in my life. My best friends' husband was helping me move and a quick sexual encounter occurred. I was riddled with guilt and shame that stayed with me. How could it have happened? On the mountain as I was reliving the event, I was shocked to find he had raped me, and I blamed myself. The clarity made me realize how fragile I was and forgave myself and the event. There were many such wakeup calls, resolutions about past relationships and more.

Tears of new wisdom came to me, and I knew that the mountain, animals and trees all played a part in the quest. There were times when I felt very weak in body and spirit, I would reach for my pipe and do my prayers to Great Spirit and let the balance of male and female be given to me through my pipe. As I smoked, I felt gratitude to all my relations. Then I felt grounded and could sleep a deep rest on my beautiful Hemlock tree.

I knew when it was time to rejoin the others. My body was drifting and needed food and water. There were no words for me to speak, only a profound silence. Little did I know the greatest lesson was still to come.

When we got back to home base, the second sweat lodge began. The moisture from steam and rocks warmed me and I thought it completed me until I realized that my pipe had slipped out of its bag on the mountain. My heart sank as the Oregon rain started pouring down. I saw my pipe on the mountain, but where?

The drive back up was a blur. I was pulling in my focus by doing a prayer to Great Spirit that I would honor myself and my pipe more than I ever had if I were guided to the spot where it had dropped. The grass was high and wet as I slowly walked step by step remembering where I had gone. A calm came over me as I approached the same Hemlock tree. As I walked up to it, I reached down in the tall grass and there was my bowl and the shaft four inches from it. It had fallen as I slid down from my tree.

A voice began speaking to me in rhyme:

> *When wisdom came, forgiveness reigns*
> *A quiet mind so I can hear when spirits near*
> *A prayer for peace, each day release.*

My heart was full of gratitude for Cougar Mountain and my journey into myself.

Shenayda Linda Deane

Shenayda's joy is music, singing and listening to the creative process in action. Her deepest desire is for all of humanity to heal through the holistic integration of mind, body and spirit. Shenayda taught at the accredited private college of The Southwest Institute of Healing Arts for 21 years.

She is a reiki master and master astrologer. Shenayda has owned the wholistic practice, Integration Therapies, in Scottsdale, AZ for the last 35 years.

Her counseling specialties are family systems and child behavior therapy as well as couple resolution. Through her practice she also offers Reiki Master Programs and Shaman training as well as a variety of classes ranging from astrology to tarot to ancient healing practices.

Phone: 602.908.6971
Website: www.shenayda.com
Email: shenayda@gmail.com
Facebook: @Integration Therapies and @Shenayda Linda Deane
Instagram: @shenaydalindadeane

Scan Me!

Song to Mother Earth

By Sophia Murphy

"Love all the earth, every ray of God's light,
every grain of sand or blade of grass, every living thing.
If you love the earth enough,
you will know the divine mystery."

~ Fyodor Dostoevsky

Chapter 41

Song to Mother Earth

By Sophia Murphy

Butterfly Being

As a quiet and shy child, I had yet to find ways to free my tender, wild spirit. I often felt like a butterfly in a cage in the outside world. When in distress, I ran to the woods behind our home and found comfort in nature and the trees. This became my sanctuary, a place where I never felt alone, shut down, or misunderstood. Grappling with the harshness of the outer world, the simple grace of nature rescued me from confusion and loneliness.

Fairies and elves were friends, and we played amongst the trees. Sitting against a tree and listening was my childhood meditation. I lay on my belly next to the brook, and the waters of the brook sang to me. I lingered outside after dark to watch the magic of lightening bugs. The sounds and scents of nature called me home. The shaking of thunder, and the fragrance of the earth after the rain enlivened me. My mother once told me that I would return from the woods changed, from feeling sad or angry into a happy child again. Nature and my family's love provided a safe nest from which to try my wings.

The time came and, mysteriously, my butterfly-self stopped beating her wings against the edges of her cage. I finally recognized the door in the cage, and it was open. My inner voice whispered, "Welcome beloved. I've been waiting for you." Grace entered and I flew through the open door, a fledgling trying her wings in the world. This poem is a reflection on the transition out of the nest:

The Lifting of Wings

Emerging from the chrysalis,
wings unfolding and stretching out as in the awakening body,
the newly winged body of the butterfly,
she intuitively knows the precise timing of this unfolding,
when to rest, wings pulsing, and
when to lift into the pure clean air...
The newness of this breathing, natural, innocent, free.
I am lifting my wings above that familiar branch
I thought was home. Looking back,
I see a temporary home, sustaining me until there was readiness
to find the next, stronger branch of life,
strong enough for my wild free spirit.

Passages

The new branch I landed on was city life, marriage, and the birth of my son. This ushered in a time of stability, joy, and greater resilience of my butterfly spirit. I found ways to begin quietly weaving my secret self into the outer world.

Then, a painful stretching of my wings. Divorce was a wrenching away from the safety of what was known. Though my inner voice said to trust myself, the pain of separation was new territory. Fear of the unknown, coupled with my wild spirit, sparked an inner flame, which remained alive inside of me. Wandering in the wilderness of non-belonging, I began hearing the call to return to the woods.

Return

After exploring city life for a few more years and protecting the one inside with delicate wings, I returned to the woods.

The first time I walked on the land, I was greeted by a wood thrush and a turtle, both assuring me that my timing was perfect. Oh, blessed peace! It was a sweet reunion with my heart and the earth. I began adjusting to the pace of nature, slowing down to a more natural rhythm of life. As I attuned to my soul through the soul of Mother Earth, I began remembering who I am. The peace of the forest helped clear the way for communion with my inner self, with earth mother, and the emergence of my natural voice. In the stillness, I was learning again how to listen to the Mother.

Seed Thoughts from Mother Nature

There is stillness in everything.

Listen for it.

Wait upon it.

When you find it, bow before it.

It is a deep pool of wonder.

How simple, how exquisite the timing is for
each heart to turn towards the light.

Out of the darkness,
the seed that was planted long ago suddenly hears its name called.

The precise moment. The perfect moment.

The moment when the golden light of sunset
is just right and frames your face before it slips quietly into dusk.

Dusk, when the light fades into the presence between worlds,
when the whippoorwill's call opens the veil.

The veil opens into the numinous,
calling the beings who wake up from the dream as night falls.

Listen deeply, you'll hear that call inside as if the whippoorwill is
calling you.

After the call, a cessation, all of nature taking
a deep inbreath in the stillness.
Then, the outbreath, the heartbeat resumes,
with the humming wild spirit of the night kingdoms.
Dusk itself crosses through the veil into the light of night.
In the light of night, you see beyond the meaning the mind searches for
in the light of day. Your unbound spirit speaks:
"Follow me!" I follow into the forest;
luminous beings show me a reflection of my soul
in a deep pool of wonder.
Be not afraid of the shiver in your spine, a recognition
of something precious beyond words.
Let the mind relax and move your being into a state of emptiness.
Receive the message
from beyond, from your soul.
A presence in the stillness nourishes, fills the soul.
The aching loneliness, sadness and regret
ever so gently take their leave. In their place,
a tenderness for all life arises.
Listening deeply,
I rest in the sacred stillness
that I am.
There is a familiar comfort,
a belonging here,
as if entering the womb of The Mother.
The longing in my soul, quieted,
my thirst quenched,
I am One.
I am.

Quiet days and nights pass. My feet are now planted firmly on the
earth. The humming in nature soothes my soul. A natural spring in the

hollow below my home has a small wishing pool, where I meditate with the dragonflies and tadpoles. The butterfly in me has stronger wings now. The feeling of belonging to Mother Earth and a nourished connection with myself has opened new ways of being in the world, replacing loneliness with a sense of wholeness.

A Song of Rebirth

Mother Earth, spirit of wholeness, receive me now,
your new child of love,
birthed through the cloudless sky in the universe of your womb,
lifted lightly into new being by the strength of your love.

Dedicated with deep gratitude to Mother Earth, Gaia, and the Divine Mother of all life, of all the Love that ever was, is, and ever will be.

Sophia Murphy

Sophia grew up in a small university town in Missouri with half academic, half country folk, which suited her curious and down-to-earth nature. As a child, her favorite playground was the woods, where she spent many wonderful hours observing all the splendid details of nature and feeling its aliveness. From those early days, Sofia developed a relationship with nature that continues to nourish and inspire her life and her poetry.

While Sophia has had a varied career, including teaching, social work, and counseling, she has never wavered from reading and writing poetry in her leisure time. Sophia's writing reflects on the deeply interwoven spirituality between the earth and humanity.

In 2016, Sofia began channeling the Ascended Masters, and is currently working on a book of divine messages from the Masters, as well as a book of poetry on finding the divine in the ordinary.

Today, Sophia is doing what she loves best—channeling spiritual messages, providing spiritual guidance and readings, writing poetry, and walking in nature. Connections with her son, grandchildren, and sisters bring her much love and joy, and increase the wellspring of wisdom in her life. She lives in the high desert of New Mexico with her two beloved cats, Chessie and Sita.

sophiawmurphy9@gmail.com
Sofia's channeling and poetry can be found here:
Facebook: Sophia: Messages of Light
Blog: willowsophia9.blogspot.com /A Path of Light

Wrinkles

By Summer D. Payne MSW, MBA

"Every setback is your setup for your comeback."

~ Joel Osteen

Chapter 42

Wrinkles

By Summer D. Payne MSW, MBA

How do I press through this WRINKLE of Divorce? When does this WRINKLE of Depression end? How can I nourish to end this WRINKLE of Disappointment? Can I Heal this WRINKLE of Cancer?

I watched her thin frail arms, with skin flappy as she slowly pushed her wheelchair closer. Carmen started to reach her hand deliberately toward the flower. As I pressed the shutter of the camera, I captured the beauty of the crevices of the wrinkles painted on her hands. As I stared at her hands, I could see the story of this woman taking care of her 11 children. In that moment, I closed my eyes to visualize her humming as she shook the laundry to hang it on the line to dry. I smiled because I could picture her braiding one of her daughter's hair as she told the children stories while they sat at her feet.

We all have our own stories. We must understand our WRINKLES, both physical and emotional, create a storybook full of wisdom. My great aunt Etheleen at 96 years old had only a few physical WRINKLES. The ones that I remember the most were the little crow's feet in the corners of her piercing grey eyes. You see, my great aunt's little crow's feet came from her unique, hearty giggle that helped her press through the miscarriage of seven babies, a husband who was an alcoholic, and the amazing love and worry she carried for her nieces and nephews.

When people see a woman with WRINKLES, they try to connect it only to age. However, WRINKLES are the precious trophies and fingerprints that display the stories that define what we've been through. Those stories shape us to become the amazing vessel that stands before the mirror every day. We may attempt to hide our physical WRINKLES with Botox, moisturizers, or makeup, but the real WRINKLES are the emotional situations that we press through that define the woman we represent.

I remember my setback on Christmas Eve of 2012. I was being evicted from my apartment with a 2-year-old little boy. I kept this WRINKLE to myself and tried to move the things from my apartment by myself. I remember the heaviness of the dresser as I tried to ease it down the stairs. My knuckles were white, and my back cracked in half. Finally, I lost my grip, and the dresser came crashing to the ground as the sun started to go down. I sat on the top step staring at the pieces with tears distorting my vision. I mustered the strength to walk into the half-empty apartment, and Joel Osteen was blaring on the television mid-sermon. I heard the Southern aroma of these words as his sermon started to speak to my spirit, "It is darkest before dawn." At that moment, I knew this was my almost-dawn moment, and I could no longer stand in the dark alone.

I called my parents to share the WRINKLE that I was experiencing, and they told me to come home. Sometimes the dark minute that you're in can drive you back to the starting line. It may not be your parents' home necessarily, but it can be a setback in your career, a relationship, or just life. However, I learned that this particular WRINKLE was going to be one of my stories of testimony. Sometimes our TEST is not for us. It can be for that person who felt like giving up, but became encouraged by witnessing your perseverance during your WRINKLE.

After I stayed with my parents, it fueled me to get my finances together. Three months later, God planted me and my son in a bigger home for less cost than that apartment. I shed tears over the Christmas Eve of being evicted. However, years later I was able to encourage another single mother on the verge of homelessness by sharing my story. That day, she made a decision to not commit suicide, and six months later was able to purchase a home.

God gave me the ministry to start WRINKLES Society of Hope. I never imagined that the YouTube channel would bring WRINKLES Warriors to pour out their stories of truth. So many testimonials of encouragement have come from stories like pastor's wife Kimberly Walker. She spoke about her faith being shaken when she was diagnosed with Trigeminal Neuralgia, a painful illness. Also, stories like the (K)ourageous strength that Ceclia Zarate shared for her battle with bipolar depression and pressing through the grief of losing her mother.

Women are superheroes who have kept their homes, community, and nation going (when men wanted to give up). There were women sewing flags and working on the farm while our men went off to war. There are currently women who decide to fight for this country who still have to face sexual trauma. Every day as a woman, we continue to rejoice and provide encouragement to those around us who may need our support. We feed our families with the nourishment of food and our unconditional love. While doing all of that, we continue to stand tall and (K)ourageous. We continue to be (K)ourageous when kneeling to say a prayer for our children, kneading bread to feed those who need food, and knitting clothing for those who are cold. Our life encouraging stories provide a beacon of light for those women who may feel that the darkness before the dawn is permanent.

Women with your WRINKLES, it's time to see that the victory is right within you! We have continuously placed ourselves on the shelf and closed the closet door. The natural caregiver's role has overtaken some women who still have dreams but have put their dreams on hold. Open that closet door back up and look at the woman you see. Put her before the children, the career, the husband and grab her off that shelf and take a good look! You may want to revisit some of those past dreams, or you may want to shine her up and make some new lines in the paint. Don't be afraid to see that woman who may have a few WRINKLES. It's not over because that WRINKLE of Breast Cancer took two things that will not define your beauty. Remember:

I am Woman, and I came to whisper, yell, or shout it from every corner of the world.

As I close, I present a special plea. Do not blow that whistle or forfeit hope. Women are a society of hope. We are women of strength who will get through it all by caring enough to share our stories with others. You have to hold on to hope that the sun is rising on your internal WRINKLES and wear your outer WRINKLES as a badge of honor.

Summer Denise Payne

My name is Summer Denise Payne, and I was born and raised in Eloy, Arizona. I am a mother of two talented young boys. My father and mother have been blessed to pastor a church for 25 years. I obtained my Bachelor's Degree in Psychology from Grambling State University in Louisiana in 2001.

I traveled back to Arizona and started my career in social work. I was able to gain my first Master's degree in Social Work from Arizona State University. I then completed a second Master's degree in Business in Health Care Administration from Columbia Southern University in Alabama in 2013.

I've worked in many facets of social work, including long-term care, hospice care, behavioral health, adoptions, and hospital social work. The ability to help others has brought me so much joy in my career growth. Now, I have poured my passion into my non-profit agency called WRINKLES Society of Hope.

My organization provides encouragement, motivation, and mentorship to women and teen-aged girls. Our WRINKLES women care enough to share their stories to encourage others to understand that the WRINKLES in our lives are temporary setbacks, which are actually a set-up for a comeback! My YouTube Channel has provided specific topics where women can hear about other women who have successfully pressed through their WRINKLES only to become stronger.

My desire is to uplift women to build a community of WRINKLES Warriors.

https://wrinklessocietyofhope.org/
https://www.youtube.com/channel/UCOEZ_vYixkkK06fIPFq-kFQ

Scan Me!

Filling the Void

By Theresa Raquel Chavez

*"Only when we become comfortable with 'not knowing'
- will we finally come to a true understanding."*

~ (Theresa Raquel Chavez – 2017)

Chapter 43

Filling the Void

By Theresa Raquel Chavez

To take back your life means to take back yourself within your life first; when we take a step back and dissect all that does not feel within alignment, and/or, what we are outsourcing to other people/things (i.e., drugs, alcohol, gambling, food, etc.), we come to realize how detached from ourselves we truly are and how we've allowed these outside forces dictate to us, the truth of who we are and the life we experience.

In the womb, we are dictated to – what we are exposed to, and the nutrients/substance/energy we receive/consume. They dream of experiences and dictate how we are supposed to perceive those same experiences, and when we are born, the battle begins – as life in the physical world begins. When we are born, we are at the mercy of those we call our parents and family. It is through these dynamics and interactions that we learn how to be part of the community that surrounds us – if this foundation is self-serving in nature, self-defeating behaviors are born, as we learn to live for those around us rather than living for ourselves.

From the moment of conception, our path is designed but so is the battle line and fight for the right to walk that path within full alignment to the truth of who we are. The moment our parent's dream of having children, they set a template as to what it all looks like and how we are supposed to fill specific voids within their own being.

I faced the ultimate consequence for this in 2014; I had a near-death experience that awoken me to myself – where my sense of self was jolted back into action. The slumbering wolf was no longer sleeping – very much so awake and more focused than ever before. During this experience, though, I felt no fear, I felt a great inner peace, and I felt in complete surrender – I did not struggle or fight, I leaned into it with my hands at my side, palms facing forward, and then everything goes black. The next thing I remember, I am on the bed, telling myself to take small breaths until I can take deeper breaths again – the manner in which my ex-husband chose to assault me was strangulation.

When I came back, I was no longer able to go against the truth of who I am, and I no longer feared him – I saw him for the truth of who he was too, and that man lives in a hell I couldn't create on my worst day. I stayed with him for a little over a year after that, consciously getting to know myself and work on things that were learned behaviors I adopted to survive. I began to heal myself and gather all my power back – he was no longer in control of me, and when I would not engage the fights anymore, no matter what he did to try to provoke me, he left, and that is when the real battle began. When we separated, I could not believe how badly I wanted to fight for our marriage – like I truly could not believe I still had anything inside me that wanted that to continue.

After we separated, I really dove deep – I threw myself into my healing, spirit, and what I call 'spiritual boot camp' where I learned how to utilize my spiritual gifts. It was shortly after he left that I had a memory come to me during meditation, where I was a light being, surrounded by other light beings who call themselves 'the council' – I felt as though we were having a briefing, where I was explaining what was going on and they asked me to come back. At first, I told them

'No' and stood strong until they left, later having two of them return and explain to me why they needed me to come back – at which point, I defeatedly agreed.

It was after this memory, that I realized what had happened that night when things went black and why I felt so at peace – all a sudden it made sense, why I did not feel like I was suffocating while I was being strangled. I literally did not feel any of the trauma because I was not present to feel it – that was the moment I had the meeting with the council.

From that moment forward, I couldn't help but notice the cyclical patterns throughout my life – moments in time where I faced the same situations with different people and I could no longer ignore the insanity, so I changed my stance in each pattern I faced until I realized, simple accountability goes an incredibly long way, and we step into congruency, we no longer have to physically engage in the patterns – as we no longer walk the path of self-evasion.

I came to realize that to refuse accountability is to evade ourselves entirely; only when we embrace and own our choices, will we step into the glorious truth of who we are – breaking the chains and freeing ourselves from the illusion that is perpetuated by the distortion we tell ourselves. We no longer wander alone in the darkness consuming the poison that has been provided to us…but rather live and lead a life of virtue, authenticity, integrity, and truth – leading to complete congruency.

When we take accountability, we realize we are the dictators of our own sovereign being/entity – where we take the bull by the horns, own our choices, and forge the path we are meant to walk, not the one everyone wants us to walk for them but the one we were meant to walk for ourselves. Because we are all one, when we walk the path for ourselves, we are walking for the collective at large – not simply temporarily filling a void for one simple person but sustaining the being that is the whole collective and healing the gaping wound that is the void.

The void that everyone is trying to fill is simply the self and life we keep evading – I cannot say this anymore straightforward – we cannot fill any other person's void, for it is our own life that needs to be filled with our own being, as it is our own void that needs to be fed and no matter how many people we put in the position to fill this void for ourselves. The void does not wish to feed on snacks such as habits, patterns, and addictions but rather feast on achievement, congruency, and intentional experience; for when we are content - the void is full, and we are whole, we ARE showing up for the collective at large.

Taking accountability is not the same as taking the blame; take on no shame, love the self, stand tall and step into the self – for you have been waiting a long time to reunite with the only true 'one who got away,' it is time.

Theresa Raquel Chavez

Theresa Raquel Chavez was born and raised in Phoenix, Arizona, with a passion instilled in her that can make the heat quiver. She is undeniably a skilled forger of paths, having worked amongst the men in the construction field as an electrician – now working for herself in collaboration with both men and women – as she has balanced her own inner masculine and feminine.

While Theresa was born with her eyes open, she experienced a near-death experience in 2014, at the hands of her ex-husband where she left her body and met with "The Council," she was asked to come back to fulfill her mission/purpose, which propelled her forward upon arrival back into the body.

Theresa is a certified reiki practitioner (master level) and coach for spiritual warriors – she not only studied the essentials but also practices them in daily life. She is an awakened multidimensional being, consciously doing her part by not only teaching but ultimately learning further from every encounter. She works closely with her guides to give each person she encounters their own personal guidance, uniquely translated to/for that specific person.

Getting in touch with Theresa

Website: https://spiritual-bootcamp.business.site/?m=true
Email: wykdluv.sbc777@gmail.com
Facebook: https://www.facebook.com/WykdLuv

Scan Me!

There Are Angels Afoot

By Tracy Boen

"With this moment I wish for you,
That every day starts with hope,
And every day ends with peace"

~ Tracy Boen

Chapter 44

There Are Angels Afoot

By Tracy Boen

Darkness and the headlights of the semi-trailer were the only things visible. The semi was closer than I had anticipated; I could hear the diesel engine and the tires screeching on the road. The sound of the air horn raced through my body. Screaming was the last thing I heard.

In the middle of the night, I woke up to my own scream, totally disoriented. I could hear Steve saying, "Are you all right?" Our dogs were frantically barking, and I could hear the horses in the distance calling to each other. This was the third night in a row I had this terrible nightmare. The intensity and realism of it had frightened me into a state of alarm.

In the morning, my thoughts were consumed with the reasons I was having the same dream. Was it caused by stress, not drinking enough water, an allergic reaction to food, or having a mental breakdown? It all seemed out of my control, but I could control not driving. For ten days, I didn't drive. I walked or rode my bike to go shopping and do my errands. Slowly, fear was replaced with calm, and driving crept back into my routine.

It was midday, and I was headed south on the 51 Piestewa Free-way to pick up an accounting project. Entering the I-10 from the on-ramp was uneventful. In an instant, everything changed. I could feel the low-pressure pull from the semi as it entered the lane next to my truck. I felt rigid and looked over at a massive spool of ground cable on its trailer. Suddenly, I saw the chain break. I hit the brakes so hard I could feel the rear end of the truck bounce. Time slowed; I experi-enced everything in slow motion. I could hear the faint sounds of a car honking. From the corner of my eye, I saw the green spool of cable larger than my truck airborne, coming towards me. It was oddly sur-real witnessing the event that was going to end my life. I estimated it was 6 inches away from my truck, just higher than the hood.

A blinding white light hit me right in the eyes, completely cover-ing the windshield. Turning my head away, I noticed the edge of the light appeared to be tips of white feathers. Time seemed to regain its normal speed. I looked out the windshield, and the spool was going uphill on the off-ramp for 7th Street, rolling almost to the intersec-tion light. It lost its momentum and headed downhill towards me yet again. I knew I had to get out of the truck. I couldn't get my seatbelt unbuckled! I watched it roll downhill as my brain tried to calculate its path. The seatbelt finally let loose, and I grabbed the door handle-only to hear the word "stay" spoken in a very direct tone. The spool paused and fell over onto the dirt landscaping before reaching the bottom of the ramp.

Every car on the freeway had stopped. The semi-trailer's cab was crushed by the spool loaded in the front of the trailer. The driver was standing outside of the truck, looking in the direction of the second spool lying in the landscaping. Everyone was okay. I called 911 to try to explain there was an accident on the I-10 going west. I barely remembered my name, and I couldn't remember my phone number. I drove up the off-ramp to Seventh Street, which just moments ago the spool had occupied. At the light, tears started rolling down my face. I made it to my client's studio to pick up the accounting. My client,

Dave, could clearly see I was in shock. He gave me bottled water, had me sit down and tell him what happened. I will always be forever grateful to Dave for taking the time from his busy schedule to hold space for me at that moment.

For me, this incident was real evidence that angels and the spirit world existed simultaneously to our earthly lives. It was no longer a question of faith or fantasy that the angelic realm is a thriving part of existence. You might be surprised at the number of times you've actually interacted with an angel! Let me give you some signs that you may recognize. You encountered a person who was very helpful in a particular situation. You sensed that he/she was "different," but you just couldn't put your finger on what made them novel. Later, when you recalled the kindness and the ease felt in the moment, you may have also recalled they were dressed differently; they carried themselves in a relaxed, comfortable manner. And the biggest of the telltale signs is that no one else was ever around when you were talking to them.

There is a reason they're called Guardian Angels! They are forever protecting and supporting our well-being. Reach out to the Angels when you need help or guidance. Just ask!

Tracy A Boen

My life has been on this amazing creative destructive cycle of changes. It has felt like holding an important bowl of water while simultaneously moving from one pillar of change to the next pillar of change without spilling any water. Though I have not lost my footing on any of the pillars, I have lost some precious water.

The last two years I have spent in meditation instructor training have been quite an undertaking, far more internally challenging than I anticipated. Of course, classes on meditation practices audio, visual, and kinetic methods and additional classes on the theories of meditation, the current scientific research results on meditation, healthy living, medical sociology, anatomy and medical terminology, the role of energy medicine in healing and studying several different cultures that are deeply rooted in the practice of meditation. I graduated with honors (Phi Theta Kappa), but even that was with a narrow margin.

The next undertaking is a physical move. Moving seems evident in light of all the internal changes in my life. This will be an enormous undertaking moving our entire lives, the horse sanctuary, and my healing practice. I feel the calling of a new place filled with love, harmony, and peace for us but especially for the horses.

In the meantime, I will be working on a new website. I will be resuming workshops and classes after we are completely moved. I will still be providing healing sessions for my long-time clients and limited physician referrals.

Tracy A. Boen
Magic Peddler, Healer, Mentor
www.GatheringEnergywithTracy.com

Ancient Intergalactic Wisdom – Journey of an Arcturian Hybrid

By Viviane Chauvet

"Together, we are far more powerful than we can ever be apart."

~ Indiana Jones & The Crystal Skull (movie)

Chapter 45

Ancient Intergalactic Wisdom – Journey of an Arcturian Hybrid

By Viviane Chauvet

How can we define the essence of wisdom? Is it the grace of the heart, soul wisdom, wisdom of the ages, Universal wisdom? Vibrationally, this energy gives the ability to think and act using knowledge, experience, understanding, common sense, and insight. Fortunately, benevolent interstellar civilizations and higher Intelligence teach human beings that they are Divine Essence of Light in body consciousness. By recognizing that this is our genuine nature, we access the most incredible wisdom of all, which unlocks infinite potential as an individual expression of Prime Creator evolving within a planetary collective.

My name is Viviane Chauvet, and I am an advanced Arcturian hybrid and Arcturus High Priestess. My soul spark originates from an ancient intergalactic civilization known as the Arcturians, located in the Boötes Constellation, home of our Unified Realm – Arcturus. My star family ascended eons ago by learning from and extracting the very wisdom of our vast history. A vital aspect of enlightenment stems from our deep respect and reverence for All Life. Over millennia, we have worked in partnership with various Star Regency Councils, intergalactic councils, and the Supreme Hierarchical Council of Light in a continuous effort to serve Prime Creator. We lovingly remind everyone that while grace is an attribute of the soul, your inner divine essence speaks through wisdom and consciousness.

As a soul emanation from Arcturus, my journey to Earth began with a desire. In response to Terra's (Gaia) urgent needs for advanced sparks of Light, our Council of Elders gathered to establish the best action plan. The Earth had finally entered into its most potent ascension timeline in thousands of years. I knew in my heart that this sentient celestial being (planet) would need the purest and highest frequency to accelerate her ascension. Therefore, I volunteered to return to Earth in a unique physical embodiment, an advanced hybrid form. My mission involves anchoring light frequencies, healing people's and animals' soul matrix from 3D archetypal patterns and mental grids, and creating positive paradigm shifts to free an entire planetary system from manufactured 3D matrix-reality (and limited belief systems).

At a very young age, I recognized that I was profoundly out of this world. I knew in my being that I was in this world on assignment. As an Arcturian conduit of higher frequency, I explored my innate abilities that ranged from holographic telepathic communication to frequency healing. These gifts allow me to decode people's intentions and vibratory state energetically. As a child, I would observe any disharmonic statement made by adults, especially doctors who believed in their prognosis regarding my "hybrid" health. How could they assess with accuracy my physical and emotional state? In my view, it seemed illogical to let someone outside of yourself dictates the quality of your health. At school, the 3D concept of competition made no sense to me. Intuitively, I would encourage classmates and friends to come together as a cohesive group. In my heart, I knew that it would serve the greatest good of all and would best support everyone's growth.

In my early twenties, I met my first spiritual teacher, Gaby, who introduced me to the concept that "I AM" Supreme Source, an Eternal Divine Essence of Light. The sacred invocation of my "I AM" presence opened up a conscious connection to my Higher Self, including my Arcturian oversoul. In a moment of cosmic enlightenment, I realized that we all are multidimensional and holographic beings. Ultimately, our goal is to return Home to Prime Creator in our pristine eternal forms. My spiritual teacher also taught me the Art of Divination through Tarot and other intuitive methodologies, including psychic and photo readings. I could "see" her light glowing around her body and in her eyes. During an out-of-body experience, I learned that we interacted in prior incarnations, especially during an Atlantean timeline where she was my mentor and fellow high priestess. She passed away a few years later, peacefully in the solitude of her home. I will always think of one of her most "down-to-earth" pieces of wisdom: "Observe life as if you were in a laboratory and see what you learn from it."

In the early 2000s, I reached a crucial point in my spiritual growth, and my capacity to hold higher frequency had increased exponentially. According to my star family, it was time to change location and move to the desert of Arizona. The ancient grids of Arizona would trigger multiple layers of accelerated transformation. In perfect synchronicity, I took a massive leap of faith and successfully moved from Montreal to Arizona. Life, as I had known it, became an imprint in time. It would take an entire book to describe in detail what took place. Most importantly of all was how I witnessed my powerful inner transformation. My interstellar team was right, as they always are, to affirm that the ancient grids and ley lines of Arizona had mystical and transformational properties.

In 2013, I gave my first official interview for an online radio show. It was during this defining and yet graceful moment that I declared that "I am an advanced Arcturian hybrid on a planetary mission." In my mind, no one would pay much attention to an unknown woman who decided to come out of the "hybrid closet." Little did I know that we would receive over 20,000 messages, comments, and requests to connect with me. So many people worldwide felt an immediate connection to my interstellar life story. Suddenly, my soul courage and determination gave a voice to thousands of people with extraordinary experiences. I was deeply moved by the response and filled with immense gratitude, along with an abstract sensation of being overwhelmed.

Everyone is on Earth by soul design, which means that your soul contains the blueprint of your actual incarnation's purposes. We help people evolve spiritually by encoding new structures (grids) of Light, which in turn accelerate their timelines. Living in the flow removes resonance of barriers or obstacles created by the lower mind. As a gift, here is an extract of the most enlightened wisdom we can provide in this space and time.

- Transcend fear by remembering that your Light is far more powerful!
- Heal your heart from old soul wounds and release limited belief systems.
- Raise your frequency and awareness every day.
- Breathe deeply into your heart and expand its energy field.
- Tune your body to higher frequencies.
- Live consciously in Oneness with yourself and all life forms, including animals.
- Cultivate your inner Cosmic Peace – the source of your inner power.
- Understand the power of your words.
- Use the power of your mind creatively for the highest good of all.
- Accept changes with Divine Grace and ease.
- Know that the ancient core of wisdom is your soul.

- Invite your Higher Self in your sacred space and then listen.
- Claim your Sovereignty as Eternal Presence of Light!

People project complex layers of reality based on their vibratory state. As you ascend to higher consciousness, the seed of your magnificence begins to blossom into a new cosmic human design. You are the masters who have returned to Earth on a divine mission. Remember that you are loved beyond expression!

Viviane Chauvet

Originally from Canada, Viviane Chauvet is internationally recognized for her inspirational life journey as an advanced Arcturian hybrid. Viviane's healing practice and teachings inspire star seeds and lightworkers to live in Universal Oneness as sovereign Divine Essence of Light. She is a multidimensional frequency healer, galactic ambassador, trans voice channel, and Arcturus high priestess. Viviane has worked as a hybrid consultant on j3FILM award-winning second documentary "Extraordinary: The Seeding" and will be featured in their third one. Today, she is the producer and co-host of The Infinite Star Connections podcast.

Viviane has been genetically engineered by the Arcturians as a unique hybrid prototype. Her healing abilities are encoded at a DNA level to create a quantum shift in the Earth's matrix grids. Our work is designed to restore the original Divine Soul Blueprint and heal fragmentation for light-body ascension. After moving to Arizona in 2006, she went through a series of profound awakenings and energetic resets. Over several years, Viviane was trained by the Arcturians in the arts of holographic and intergalactic frequency healing. She pursued her studies with many teachers and became certified in Crystalline Soul Healing®, Unity Field Healing®, Soul Genesis™, ThetaHealing®, and QHHT®. Through her work in holographic healing, Viviane has developed the Arcturian Energy Matrix Healing® modality to attain spiritual and soul unification beyond the 3rd dimensional matrix-reality. Owner of Infinite Healing from the Stars, she also serves as an emissary for the Intergalactic Councils and other interstellar delegations.

Website: https://www.infinitehealingfromthestars.com/
Facebook: https://www.facebook.com/vivianechauvetgalactichealer
YouTube: https://www.youtube.com/c/VivianeChauvetGalacticHealer
Email: viviane@infinitehealingfromthestars.com

Scan Me!

Epilogue

Now, dearest reader, our evergreen **Wisdom** book's experiential enrichments can divinely dwell on your nightstand, at the ready to inspire, uplift and encourage you. Reveling in the authors' beautiful stories, **Guided by Grace,** continues to be transformational.

Our Writerlies created, cultivated, and cared for a community of connectivity, a deeper place where value, integrity, and courage reside.

The **Silver Sisterhood** celebrated each chapter with meaningful messages, mighty ministries, and stylized magic. From being gloriously grounded, and realistically recognizing the joys of fulfillment, to the sacred scribe, our amazing authors are luminous leaders of the heart, mind, and soul. Both brave and bold, their wisdom is treasured.

Several would-be and seasoned authors have asked to contribute to our *Wisdom of the Silver Sisters, Guiding Grace, Volume II.* As one of our existing writerlies or first time ever-to-be published authors, we honorably, cordially, and enthusiastically invite you to join us. Indeed, To Be Continued…

Write On!

In Grace & Gratitude!
Sandy Rogers
Sharyn G. Jordon
www.WisdomOfTheSilverSisters.com

We wholeheartedly welcome and accept reviews!
Please leave review on our book page on
Amazon or Goodreads

Special Acknowledgment

to
Becky Bee Norwood
Spotlight Publishing

In a virtual space where publishing platformers promise to deliver our book babies to a waiting world, it is worthwhile to know Becky Bee Norwood's wunderkind system works in real-time.

After years or perhaps months of birthing our stories into the written word and weaving our tales into chapters and verse, it is thrilling to Become Published. Trusting that our noble narratives, which are chock full of timeless wisdom, wonder-filled and worthy tales, go to print is essential. Gratefully, Becky's good standing history, keen expertise, and dependability make that possible.

Becky Bee and yes, Bee is her middle name denotes exactly what it symbolizes. Her stellar track record would exhaust the average person. Passionate about what and whom she is BEing, Becky is a waymaker, promise-keeper, and a worker-bee. Her impressive publishing accomplishments shine a light on how Becky Bee epitomizes this sacred totem. From the ancients, honeybees have represented BEing Industrious, to bring in messages from the Divine, and denotes fertility. Think of the axions associated with Bees: such as *'a hive of activity,'* and although *'busy as a bee'* is one, our Becky Bee is hardwired to BE Productive!

Since we have worked with other publishers, we know the vast difference that someone with Becky's in-depth understanding, guidance, and oversight makes. During the ***Wisdom of the Silver Sister, Guiding Grace***'s project, her innate wisdom was paramount from start to finish. Plus, her superb tools and software assisted our authors in communicating better and meeting critical deadlines. She continues to evolve her technology. Her proven method of procedures has taken over three hundred authors to Best Selling Status, many of them to International Best Seller Status. She has also developed a masterfully sustainable process for keeping her author's book babies in the public's eye.

Becky interviewed many of our Silver Sisters and created a QR code that opens up a short video to tell the story behind our story. We Silver Sisters are forever grateful for Becky's unsurpassed professionalism, big heart, and unyielding perseverance. She is BEEing the Change!

In Grace and Gratitude,
Sandy Rogers & Sharyn G. Jordan

The End

Manufactured by Amazon.ca
Bolton, ON

23251386R00216